Published in Great Britain in 2006 by Wiley-Academy,
a division of John Wiley & Sons Ltd

Copyright © 2006

John Wiley & Sons Ltd, The Atrium, Southern Gate, Chichester,
West Sussex, PO19 8SQ, England
Telephone (+44) 1243 779777

Email (for orders and customer service enquires): cs-books@wiley.co.uk
Visit our Home Page on www.wiley.co.uk or www.wiley.com

Executive Commissioning Editor: Helen Castle
Development Editor: Mariangela Palazzi-Williams
Content Editor: Louise Porter
Publishing Assistant: Calver Lezama

Other Wiley Editorial Offices

John Wiley & Sons Inc., 111 River Street, Hoboken, NJ 07030, USA

Jossey-Bass, 989 Market Street, San Francisco, CA 94103-1741, USA

Wiley-VCH Verlag GmbH, Boschstr. 12, D-69469 Weinheim, Germany

John Wiley & Sons Australia Ltd, 42 McDougall Street, Milton,
Queensland 4064, Australia

John Wiley & Sons (Asia) Pte Ltd, 2 Clementi Loop #02-01, Jin Xing Distripark,
Singapore 129809

John Wiley & Sons Canada Ltd, 22 Worcester Road, Etobicoke,
Ontario, Canada M9W 1L1

ISBN-13 978 0 470 01743 2 (HB)
ISBN-10 0 470 01743 0 (HB)

Page design and layouts by Jeremy Tilston
Printed and bound by Conti Tipocolor, Italy

Modern Family Gardens

Caroline Tilston   Photography **Juliette Wade**

Contents

For Claire, Sue, Richard and Richard
who went out of their way to
encourage and help me.

Introduction

The title *Modern Family Gardens* was decided on early in the process of writing this book. But it has led to some discussion. What makes a family? And what is modern? When going through the gardens feature, I asked myself these two questions, and came to the following conclusions.

Firstly, I cannot comment on what makes a 'family', though it does involve certain competing demands on the garden. Whenever two or more people are creating a garden together, there will be different influences and needs. And, of course, the implication of the word 'family' is that there are children about. However, it is important to make clear that the 'modern family gardens' featured in this book are not children's gardens; they are gardens that

cater to the needs of both parents and children. What is remarkable is the diversity of ways in which the designers and families involved have chosen to satisfy these different demands. But what all of them have in common is that they have created stunning gardens that work for what the family needs from the space. Throughout the book I have attempted to make these design issues and their solutions understandable so that they may be transferable to other gardens.

Secondly, I have taken the view (perhaps bravely) that what is 'modern' is that which is being created now. Good design is more important than any specific use of modern materials or prescriptive design routes. In the very process of making a garden to meet the various needs of the family, its creators are tackling the garden in a modern way. This needs-led design mirrors what has already happened inside the house, where living spaces have been opened up so that people interact more closely. So the garden has been opened up to the house, and a new informality in the way the spaces are used has emerged. The variety of needs, and how they have been met in design briefs in such a myriad of ways, is exciting, and should not be curtailed by preconceived ideas of what counts as a 'modern' garden.

What is clear from the two issues above is that gardens are spaces to be used and enjoyed, taking into account both the opportunities and constraints of a particular site as well as the needs and wishes of its occupants – an approach that treats the garden as an 'outside room'.

The outside room

The concept of an 'outside room' takes gardens away from gardening. The garden is somewhere to sit, to play and to enjoy, which can also be decorated and furnished, just like any other room. It opens up the outside space for all to enjoy, whether or not they know a zinnia from a zantedeschia. The space is there for you and your family and needs to work for you. You don not work for it.

I have to admit that the idea of the garden as an outside room has become something of a cliché. However, as with most clichés, it is useful and based on some truth. Perhaps the problem I have with it is that it denigrates gardens. It downplays their importance.

If a garden is just an outside room, it is on a par with a sitting room or playroom. But a garden is much more than that.

For a start, it is outside. It is a place you can fill with greenery and create a whole, natural environment. For adults this can be a wonderful refuge and a place to connect with nature. For children, being outside is vital to their well-being and development (see box on page 11).

Gardens are usually, though not always, larger than most rooms within the home, so both adults and children can lose themselves in them, hide away and escape from the 'real' world.

Gardens also offer the potential to create your own world. This is another way in which the garden is more than 'just another room'. The possibilities for developing the space are much more exciting: lighting, sound systems and heating, walls and water features are just some of the flood of recent ideas that are encouraging people to realise the potential of their gardens. More than any room inside the house, the outdoor room allows you to express yourself and to create something special. Gardening programmes on television, and garden shows, are demonstrating that what was once exceptional is now possible and achievable.

This ignition of interest and demand for better gardens means that more money and more time are now being spent on them. Designers and contractors are responding with increasingly inventive and unusual structures, and more

innovative uses of materials. The potential for construction and effects seems endless. All of this means the garden can be a truly inviting environment that can be moulded to individual tastes and needs, whether a minimalist, calming space, a Moroccan courtyard, an Italianate heaven or a jungle. This is what sets gardens apart.

So, if gardens are becoming more important to adults, how much more significant are they for children? For many of us, gardens and outdoor spaces represent some of our strongest childhood memories. The world seemed huge

ABOVE: Jungle-like planting can make even tiny spaces amazing, adventurous places for children.

OPPOSITE: The huge glass doors typical of many new extensions blur the distinction between inside and out.

and filled with opportunities for excitement. The new, open-minded, can-do approach to gardens is ideal for creating wonderful places to play for our own children that will leave them with similar lasting memories.

When a garden is interesting, well thought out and beautiful, children will appreciate it. They might not comment on the great use of structure and texture, but they will find more to enjoy. Compare the wonderfully interesting gardens of today with traditional suburban gardens of the past, with their central lawn and narrow surrounding beds. If you were a child, which would you rather play in? So, even without an iota of compromise, modern gardens are already well ahead when it comes to being child-friendly and stimulating.

The importance of play for children

Children's lives are today structured in ways that would not have been dreamt of even just 20 years ago. After-school care and increased take-up of out-of-school activities mean that time to just 'muck about' is now severely limited. Doug Cole, Chair of the International Play Association (IPA), describes this as 'play malnourishment'. He believes that children are being deprived of play: 'Play is what children do, it is what they are, it is their way of making sense of the world around them.' Deprived of the chance to play, he goes on, 'children's behaviour, neurological development and social development all suffer.'

Researchers have also looked into where play is best carried out. You will not be surprised to hear that outside, in the open air and engaging with nature, provides the best environment for all-round play. Children are able to explore, observe, engage and manipulate their environments, and develop both imaginatively and socially much more readily in an outdoor setting.

However, despite all this research, children's environments are becoming increasingly more limited. At some point in the 1980s, their worlds began to close in. Parents' fears of traffic, strangers and physical hazards have resulted in a loss of freedom for children that, for previous generations, was taken for granted. This change in attitudes was starkly shown in 1990 by M Hillman, J Adams and J Whitelegg in their *One False Move: A Study of Children's Independent Mobility*: between 1970 and 1990, the number of seven- and eight-year-olds allowed to travel to school on their own dropped from 80 per cent to just 9 per cent.

This goes some way to emphasising why the garden environment is so important for children. If they need outdoor play in order to develop socially, cognitively and emotionally, but social attitudes will not let them wander, one of the few places left is the garden.

The good news is that developmental theorists are now realising that children do not need a lot of space to enjoy and engage with their environment. Psychologists once believed that one of the main reasons for play was to burn off 'surplus energy', which, incidentally, is one of the reasons why school playgrounds tend to be such huge open spaces. However, it is now acknowledged that play at the micro level is just as important – hiding away, building a den, watching worms. So, if your garden is not big enough for even half a football pitch, it can still provide a wonderful environment for children's play.

LEFT TO RIGHT: Water can provide endless fun for children, and moving, shallow water, such as in the water feature here, is ideal for tiny ones; From the perspective of a two-year-old, a simple path through plants is an adventure into the unknown; Climbing frames are especially useful where lots of children play together, as there is no need to wait in turn.

The gardens

It is not just the demands of users that govern the design of a garden. The nature of the garden itself can also place limitations on – or create opportunities for – the design. These are often garden-specific; for example, a garden may be designed to make the most of a good view. However, this is not going to be terribly useful for many readers of this book, so what I have tried to do with each of the gardens featured is to bring out those elements that will be most relevant and most useful to as many people as possible – for example, dealing with changes in level, creating sitting areas, dividing up space and finding low-maintenance plants.

One of the most important factors in garden design is size, and I have used this to divide the book into sections. Although ideas appropriate for larger gardens will often translate to smaller spaces – the lit-up rill running around the periphery of the country garden can be just as effective in a tiny city garden – size nevertheless has an inevitable impact on how the space can be used. A number of the larger gardens in the book include features specifically for children, such

OPPOSITE TOP: Beautiful views such as this are a rare and wonderful find in gardens. This one has been cleverly enhanced with carefully pruned trees and hedges.

OPPOSITE BELOW: Even in very large gardens, there are often smaller areas that can be translated into more intimate spaces. Two chairs, looking out over the lawn, add to the view, even if there is no time to sit in them.

BELOW: Enchanting avenues are as appealing to children as they are to adults.

as climbing frames, swings and trampolines, which work within the overall design without infringing upon it. In contrast, for very small gardens, the best design solution is often to keep the space as open as possible to allow for different uses at different times. The larger the garden, the easier it is to meet different demands. Areas can be separated off for children and adults, and both can have a variety of different environments to enjoy.

But the true heart of a family garden is often the shared space – the hidden seating areas and the eating areas that can be enjoyed by all ages. It is this integration of needs that makes the gardens in this book contemporary. In the past, gardens were for adults. More recently, a token play frame has been added. But now a new feeling of joint adventure is taking over. What is a wonderful hidden den for children is used by adults for their work. A secret path is as delightful to children as it is to their parents. People are seeing the benefits of investing in gardens and creating the gardens they want, the gardens their children want and, indeed, the gardens they wanted when they were young.

Family gardens: a brief history

The moneyed have always had fun with their gardens. From the tumbling water gardens at Villa Lante in Italy to the creations by Le Nôtre for the French court and the elegant estates of the English aristocracy, gardens like these expressed the feelings of the Establishment, announcing their aspirations and expectations. It was the aristocrats and the Church who had the money, and so led the way in landscape design.

Even after the Industrial Revolution, when new money came from banking and trade, the gardens these nouveau riche created tended to hark back to early times or traditional ideas of Eden. By the beginning of the 20th century, individuals such as Lionel de Rothschild at Exbury, and Huttleston Broughton at Anglesey Abbey, began creating their own gardens, though very much in line with tradition. Further down the social scale, most people's disposable incomes did not stretch to experimentation in their gardens – not yet, anyway.

Change came about after the Second World War. New housing developments and an increase in home ownership led to an increased interest in improving homes and gardens. As Jane Fearnley-Whittingstall says in her book *The Garden: An English Love Affair – One Thousand Years of Gardening*: 'Gardens looked inwards again, as they had in medieval times, attempting to exclude a hostile world and to give privacy from prying neighbours. Behind the walls and fences, the privet hedges and the dripping laurels most gardens had no exciting secrets to hide.'

Pleasure from these postwar gardens still came from plants. Gardens were for gardening, and 'garden design' for the masses was yet to be invented. But then came the 1960s – the start of a revolution. Newly opened garden centres lit the consumerist flame in gardeners: one could now buy plants on a whim without having to order from a catalogue. And not just plants. The centres also sold containers and, increasingly, water features, pergolas and everything else you needed to 'do' your garden. Garden designer John Brookes came along with an entirely new way of looking at spaces, bringing design to England's middle-classes, in his book *Room Outside: A New Approach to Garden Design*. Gardens were no longer about muck and weeds and propagation – they were places to be enjoyed and decorated.

Forty years later, that revolution is still continuing, being pushed further and further to new extremes where outside rooms no longer need plants, where the idea of 'gardening' is totally alien, and where we have garden-makeover programmes that promise an entirely new garden in just 30 minutes.

There are purists who throw up their hands in horror at this. The art of gardening, the knowledge of gardening, the hands-on work of gardening are becoming obsolete, they say. But gardening is a hobby, and it would be unreasonable to expect every householder with a garden to enjoy it. At least with the new 'low-maintenance' designer gardens, people are out there enjoying the space and creating new and exciting areas that may have otherwise been just dead ground. This is what is so wonderful about the changes happening now. People have the time, money and opportunity to have fun with their gardens and, just as the aristocrats did in the past, they are creating their own ideas of paradise.

TOP: Sandpits are a great idea for children, but some toddlers will eat anything, and need to be watched carefully.

BOTTOM: Even children who can swim can get into difficulties if there is no easy way out of the water.

Safety

I have not included much in the book about safety. I think parents know their own children and know the risks they feel are acceptable for their children to be exposed to. That level of risk will be different for each child, and will inevitably change over time, so it is difficult to give blanket warnings. However, two things I am paranoid about – mainly because the damage can be terminal – are cars and water. I was interviewing TV gardening presenter Kim Wilde a while back, and she told me the following story. There was a little girl in her garden who leant into a bucket half full of water, lost her footing, fell head first into the bucket and could not get back out. Fortunately the girl was being watched. But how many of us would think a bucket of water could pose a threat?

Reference section

The reference section at the end of the book includes a list of selected useful, easy-to-grow plants that draw on all of the planting trends mentioned in the main chapters. There is also a directory giving contact details for all of the designers and suppliers referred to in the main part of the book, and for the public gardens featured, as well as sources of advice. A separate Further Reading section lists books referred to in the chapters, as well as a number of others you may find useful.

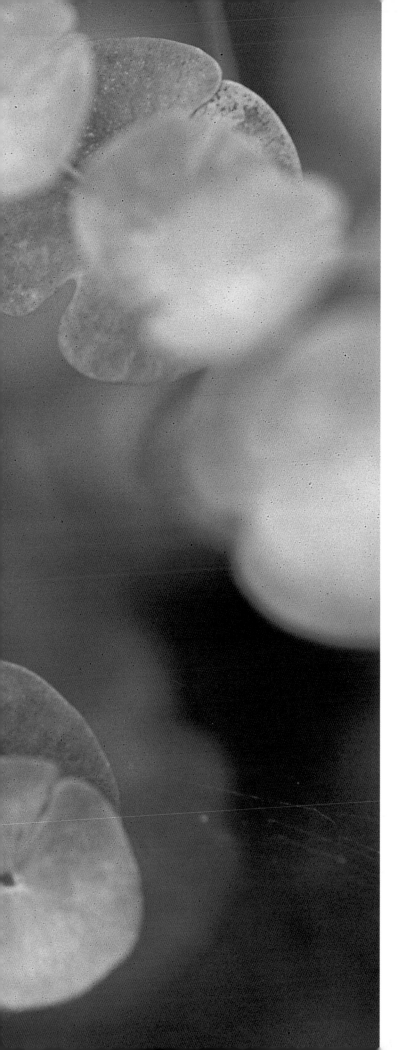

Extra Small

XS Introduction

Tiny spaces present special challenges when trying to create a garden, but there is no area in which a garden cannot be made. Even if the area is too small to step into, it can be decorated to create a beautiful view. If there is no soil, containers can be put on walls or on the floor. And if there is little light, there are plants that thrive in shady places, and artificial lights can brighten things up. Looking at it this way, if you have a space that is large enough to walk into you are doing well, and if you have a space where you can sit as well, you have grounds.

The gardens in this section fall into this category: big enough to walk into and sit in, but not much bigger. They are one-room affairs. However, what they demonstrate is that, in garden design, there is a variety of ways to tackle tiny spaces, from stark minimalism, to orientalism, to a leafy jungle.

Despite the apparent differences between them, they do have several things in common that can help with the laying out of any tiny space.

Strong design

Each has a very strong layout and, in a way, a formality. This is a good starting point. In a tiny space, formality of some kind is best. I am sure there must be a way to do a tiny garden informally and for it to work, but I cannot think of one. In all of the gardens in this section, the layout is very clear and defined, lines are straight, and there is a balance, if not symmetry, to the geography.

Using all available space

There cannot be any 'dead' areas in tiny gardens like these. Everything is on view, and all the available space needs to be used. Putting up a wall, as in the Green and White garden, provides an area behind which to hide playthings, but, even here, a sitting area has been squeezed in to make use of what could have been just a storage area.

A clear area

The starting point of all the designs in this chapter is a clear, open space for sitting, with the surrounds then filled with planting. Even though each garden tackles this in a different way, space constraints mean that if you want to sit in the garden, you do need to keep an open area, and this will take up a large part of the garden. Keeping as much of the area as clear as possible also gives you the flexibility to use it in different ways.

No clutter

The gardens all have a clearly defined layout and a large space for sitting, and are also clutter free. This is very important, as tiny gardens need to be clean and clear, and will not tolerate disorder, whether in the design or in what is added later on. Inbuilt seating and storage can help to keep mess to a minimum.

Planting

Even where planting is abundant in the gardens featured in this section, it is kept at bay in clearly defined beds. The choice of planting is also very important. In tiny areas it has to work hard all year round. Many of the plants used are evergreens, as tiny gardens cannot afford to have an off-season. At one extreme is the jungle effect of the City Jungle garden in Earls Court. This is leafy with a large variety of plants filling its beds, overhanging the paths and obscuring the view. At the other extreme, the Minimalist garden uses a very limited palette of plants, chosen very carefully for their architectural qualities. Both gardens rely heavily on evergreens and structural planting, and the lines between pathways, sitting areas and planted areas are clear.

ABOVE: A strong identity, clear lines, defined beds and no clutter – a perfect design for a small garden.

Attention to finish

When designing a tiny garden, remember that every inch will get scrutinised, and every inch will get wear, so it is important to put effort into the finish.

Water features

Three of the gardens use small water features. These can lift a tiny space, creating movement and light.

Identity

The key to the successful design of the very small gardens in this section is that each has an individual identity and look. The designs do not just meet technical demands – they have a sense of place about them. Having in mind a clear identity for your garden beforehand will help to determine what materials and plants to use, and the overall look. The identity will be based on what you want to use the garden for, on your personal taste, and on the bare bones of what already exists.

Extra Small.01

Minimalist

James Lee
Chelsea, London, 2004

'In a very small space everything has to be perfect.' In this garden, the designer, James Lee, is certainly true to his word. It is a wonderful example of pared-down perfection. Everything here has a strong line and clear purpose, and all of it is beautifully executed and detailed.

The tiny space has two entrances: one from below ground, from the kitchen, and one from the living room, set slightly above the garden. The view from the kitchen is of a trained Australian ivy (*Muehlenbeckia complexa*), which does very well in this sheltered spot at the base of the stairwell.

> **Designer's tip** There is a microclimate in this little stairwell. Although there is not much sun, it is always sheltered, and the vent from the boiler means it stays well above freezing. If you have a vent like this, however, always make sure it is clear of planting.

From here, steep stairs rise up to the garden. They are beautifully finished in Italian basalt with toughened-glass and stainless-steel railings. At the top, the garden opens out into a central space.

With a tiny space like this, the designer decided it was best to leave as much of the area as possible uncluttered, making it appear larger and allowing for as much flexibility as possible for both adults and children; for example, children's toys can be brought out during the day, but cleared away later.

Space-saving features include a built-in table, on the side nearest to the house, made of the same Italian basalt as the floor. The table blends into the background so well that it is barely visible in the picture in this chapter. However, it provides a permanent eating area with storage space underneath.

The glass-and-metal fence carries on, around from the stairs, to enclose the stairwell. Behind the table, the railings are surprisingly high, but the design here is deliberate, preventing children from falling into the well should they climb on to the table. In a similar vein, an extendable stair-gate at the top of the steep stairs, made in the same materials as the rest of the fencing so that it blends into the background, ensures the stairs are not treacherous for the two little children who live here.

Along the rear of the space is a raised bed, finished on the top with the Italian basalt, again giving unity to the area. The retaining wall is at seat height and provides a long bench right along the rear of the garden. The raised bed contains black bamboo (*Phyllostachys nigra*) to give an evergreen upright screen that softens the whole area.

There are only two other types of plant in the garden. In a line along the floor is mind-your-own-business (*Soleirolia soleirolii*), which breaks up the surface of the floor and softens its impact. This is really clever. The line has been placed far enough away from the raised bed so that you do not put your feet on it when you are sitting down. And in addition, it acts as a drainage channel for the courtyard: the paving slopes down to the line, and water drains to it – the plant gets watered and there is somewhere for the water to go. Perfect.

At the top of the two steps up to the living room, a small carpet of the evergreen Lily turf (*Ophiopogon japonicus*) has been planted next to the glass fence. This balances the rest of the planting perfectly, and begins to demonstrate how minimalist gardens work. Take away this piece of planting

DESIGN BRIEF
- Contemporary minimalist
- Limited palette of hard materials
- Space to eat outside

FEATURES
- Italian basalt table
- Toughened-glass and stainless-steel fence
- Slatted cedar trellis

and the composition suddenly becomes stark and unbalanced. Only things that need to be here for use or for balance are included here – nothing more.

Designer's tip Designers talk about 'masses' and 'voids'. Voids, the spaces left, are as important to a design as what is put in. In garden design, it is relatively easy to manipulate the size, proportions and decorative feel of voids. Here, the perfect proportions for the central activity area have been created by the depth and size of the raised bed, the height of the walls and lack of clutter.

One of the most beautifully detailed pieces of the design is the cedar slatwork around the walls of the garden. Made from different thicknesses of cedar, it unifies the whole space. These boundary walls do not need to be covered with planting; they are a part of the design and can be left uncluttered. Held within them is the central, beautifully proportioned space.

Minimalism does not mean empty. The garden here could be described as a small area with a long bench, a table, and about 20 per cent of the area given over to plants – which could apply to any garden. What it has is a precise use of line, a carefully thought out integration of function and form, and a balance to its design that gives it stability and strength. It is so clean, so clear, that the lack of space does not matter. Indeed, this stark minimalism would not work so well in a larger garden.

ABOVE: Toughened-glass and stainless-steel railings are safe for children and stunning to look at.

BELOW LEFT: Steep stairs finished in Italian basalt rise up to the garden.

BELOW: A line of mind-your-own-business (*Soleirolia soleirolii*) breaks up the flat surface of the floor and provides drainage for the area.

ABOVE: Clean and simple lines, a minimal palette of materials and plants and perfect proportions make a wonderful minimalist garden.

Creating a minimalist garden

Minimalist gardens are difficult to get right. There is no fudging around the edges, no room for a slight mistake – what is there has to be spot on. However, on the plus side they tend to be low maintenance and a tranquil antidote to busy lives. With roots in the Orient, minimalist gardens are places for contemplation and repose. As Shunmyo Masuno says in *The Modern Japanese Garden*, they create 'a space that provides the means for the mind to become acutely sensitive to the simple small matters that are often blanketed by daily life'.

The following are some useful tips for creating a minimalist garden:

- Remove all unnecessaries and decoration from the design. The elements must be 'condensed to the essentials', as architect John Pawson says. 'One of the most significant principles is to omit the unimportant, in order to emphasise the important.'
- Make a clear, strong, simple composition with what you have left.
- Think not only about what is going in, but also about the spaces left between.
- A composition that uses sharp geometry and highly structured forms is key. Mathematically ideal forms – spheres, cubes, cones and pyramids – have a calmness and harmony.
- Although minimalist does not have to mean symmetrical, symmetry gives instant order to the design. It has been found that humans biologically favour symmetry. Perhaps originally a survival mechanism, this propensity has transferred into preferences in art and in our environment.
- Repetition in the design will create a simplicity and rhythm that gives further ordering to the elements.
- Once you have worked out what is going where, unify and simplify the materials used. There are no rules for this, but in this garden, for example, there are only two basic materials – the Italian basalt used for all the hard landscaping within the garden, and cedar wood for the upright features.
- Minimalist gardens often use modern materials to give a sleek, clean line. But look at the wonderful minimalism of Japanese gardens and it becomes evident that natural materials can fit just as well with minimalist principles.
- The selection of plants should also be limited. A jungle or cottage effect is not going to create the required simplicity. Planting may even consist of just a single plant, displayed so as to be appreciated for its form rather than for its effect amongst others.

Extra Small.02

City Jungle
Debbie Roberts and Ian Smith
Earls Court, London, 2003

The garden here was overgrown and neglected when Debbie Roberts and Ian Smith, from garden-design company Acres Wild, first saw it. And it was also about to shrink: an extension was to be built out from the house and a studio planned for the far end. What was left measured only 5.5 x 10 metres (18 x 33 feet).

In this small space was a steep change in level from the entrance up to the main part of the garden. Unusually, the main access to the garden is from the basement kitchen, with the ground rising up by over a metre (3.2 feet). This meant that the main view from the kitchen could have been a forbidding wall.

Fortunately, the garden designers were brought in at an early stage so that they could work alongside the architect responsible for both the extension to the house and the studio at the rear of the garden.

It is immediately obvious that the garden here forms part of the house. The materials and the layout seamlessly flow through the whole project. The same iroko wood is used for the studio and for the decking, and the grey Cumbrian kirkstone slate on the ground outside fits perfectly with the tones used in the modern kitchen. The transition from house to garden works well. From the kitchen one is faced, not with a forbidding wall, but with elegant wide steps that invite the eye (and the body) up into the garden.

Designer's tip If you are building a house or an extension that is going to affect the garden, get the garden designer in sooner rather than later, so that architect and garden designer can work together to create an integrated, flowing space. In addition, money could be saved if, for example, machinery and manpower needed for work inside the house can be used outside too. A recent trend is for garden designers and architects to get together themselves to offer a complete design package.

Where there is a change in level like this, the ideal thing to do is to push the rise back, away from the house, so that it does not dominate the view. The steps here have been positioned far enough away from the house that they do not feel like they are falling into the basement. Also, the space created at the lower level is now large enough to be used for an outdoor dining table for family meals.

Designer's tip Stairs are always an issue when a garden is designed with small children in mind. Where there is a change in level in a smaller space, there are bound to be steps. One solution is to include a stair-gate of some sort. However, the width of the steps in the garden here meant this was not an option. It is worth remembering that stairs are a danger to children for only a few years. So, if you are designing the garden for long-term use, it might be worth putting up with the extra supervision in the early years (which you would probably do anyway with very small children), and this was the view taken by the owners of the garden here.

DESIGN BRIEF
- A city oasis
- Green in summer and winter
- Screening from neighbours
- Terrace for eating
- Access to studio at rear of garden

FEATURES
- Chequerboard pattern
- Studio at rear
- Steps up to main garden
- Cumbrian kirkstone slate

Entering the garden from a lower level is unusual. Normally, you would look upon a garden, perhaps from a slightly raised terrace, or at least from your own height. But you look up first to see this garden, and the planting at the entrance here makes the most of this. The designers have carefully chosen plants like bamboos and tree ferns (*Dicksonia antarctica*), which make a lovely pattern against the sky, and the red-leaved acer (*Acer palmatum* 'Fireglow'), which, with the light of the sky behind it, glows like stained glass.

The design of the upper level had to meet some practical considerations. The studio at the end meant that an all-weather route down through the garden was necessary. This would usually dictate a path, but, rather than a single, demarcated path there is paving along one side of the garden that blends into cobbles and planting in a chequerboard pattern.

This interesting use of hard landscaping was possible because there is no lawn. Whether or not to include a lawn in a garden this small is a major decision. In their favour, lawns are relatively low maintenance, are green all year round, and provide a soft place to sit. On the other hand, they can prove a muddy obstacle in the winter if you need access across them and they do, in general, dictate a design with a large, central flat area surrounded by planting. In addition, it can be a nuisance to have to own a lawn mower for such a small space.

Freed from all of that, the design can be both more intimate and more intricate. The chequerboard pattern is a wonderful idea. Squares of paving mingle with squares formed by the low-growing mind-your-own-business (*Soleirolia soleirolii*), but the idea really comes to life when it is formed in three dimensions. Clipped box squares (*Buxus sempervirens*) and the cube-shaped water feature give height and interest to the geometric design. The water feature has been carefully chosen. Water features often do not fit with the rest of the garden, but this one is actually part of the design and carries through the cube-and-square geometric patterns. It is made of black basalt, with water flowing up through the centre and down the sides on to loose pebbles. It is also safe for small children. The reservoir is hidden and there is no deep water above ground level.

ABOVE: Cubes of clipped box (*Buxus sempervirens*) carry through the chequerboard theme of the garden.

OPPOSITE: The new extension and the garden, both of which use grey as their base colour, work together beautfully.

The year-round green that has been lost by not having a lawn is compensated for by the evergreen, lush planting that gives an almost jungle feel to the garden. Tall plants such as the black bamboo, acers, tree ferns and castor oil (*Fatsia japonica*) plants form the walls. Lower lush planting includes calla lilies (*Zantedeschia aethiopica*), evergreen pittosporum (*Pittosporum tobira* 'Nanum'), phormiums and ferns. The planting is chosen for form and structure rather than flowers, and fits with the modern, architectural design of the garden and the new extension.

Importantly, to keep all of this lush foliage going, there is an irrigation system of leaky pipes throughout the planting.

The combination of intimate design and lush planting is essential to fulfil a major part of the brief – to create a secluded oasis, screened from neighbours. Plants crowd in to create not just screening, but atmosphere. They hide the boundaries of the garden so that its size (or lack of it) is indistinguishable.

With a small space like this it is necessary to prioritise what you want from it. The garden here is never going to be big enough to accommodate children's play areas and a retreat for adults. But there is plenty of storage at the rear for children's toys, which can be hidden away when the adults want to use the garden, and there are playgrounds nearby. What cannot be found elsewhere is privacy, seclusion and greenery.

ABOVE: Set amongst squares of mind-your-own-business (*Soleirolia soleirolii*) and cubes of box (*Buxus sempervirens*), the water feature fits perfectly into its surroundings and forms part of the geometric design.

LEFT: Geometric patterns of slate contrast with random cobbles.

BELOW: Mind-your-own-business.

RIGHT: With no deep water, the black basalt cube is safe and fun for children.

OVERLEAF: Despite the size limitations of the garden, there is no skimping on the steps, which are wide, gracious and inviting.

LEFT TO RIGHT: Tree fern (*Dicksonia antarctica*), black bamboo (*Phyllostachys nigra*) and mind-your-own-business (*Soleirolia soleirolii*).

Low-maintenance evergreens for a city jungle

The plants below are the sorts you can put in and leave. For the first year you can help them get established with extra water in dry spells, but otherwise they are the lowest of low maintenance.

Bamboos
Bamboos are happy in sun or light shade, and come in many forms. However, for low maintenance the best are those that do not spread too far, too fast. The most popular must be black bamboo (*Phyllostachys nigra*), which has black stems, and golden bamboo (*Phyllostachys aurea*), which has golden stems. For more leaves and less stem, try umbrella bamboo (*Fargesia murielae*).

Castor oil plant (*Fatsia japonica*)
Huge leaves and an ability to grow in the shadiest places make this a wonderful choice for city gardens.

Lomaria-leaved mahonia
(*Mahonia lomariifolia*)
Mahonias have a bad reputation; they are seen as 'supermarket' planting and, truth be told, they are not the most elegant plant. Nevertheless, for evergreen bulk at

the rear of the border and scent in the winter they are a good choice.

Chusan palm (*Trachycarpus fortunei*)
This is a great hardy palm – the one to go for if you are not a gardener.

Spanish dagger (*Yucca gloriosa*)
Best planted in full sun where the sharp rigid leaves make a strong statement and can cast wonderful shadows on walls or floors.

Phormium 'Platt's Black'
These have sword-like leaves from a central base. Some of the cultivars are a little garish, but this new (almost) black-leaved one is wonderful and is a great foil for lighter plants.

Black grass (*Ophiopogon planiscapus* 'Nigrescens')
This short black grass can be used to mirror, on a smaller scale, the black phormium. It can take its time to establish itself, so either buy lots or be patient.

Bressingham Ruby (Elephant's Ears – Bergenia) (*Bergenia* 'Bressingham Ruby')
You have to be a little careful with bergenias. They are smallish plants

that flower in late winter, but some of them are elephantine and ugly. However, the dark purple leaves of this one are beautiful.

Mind-your-own-business
(*Soleirolia soleirolii*)
This is a low-growing plant that will spread along cracks in paving forming a lovely green mat.

Armand clematis (*Clematis armandii*)
An evergreen climber with large leathery leaves that is happy in sun or shade, this plant also has scented flowers in spring. It will need a frame or wires to grow along.

Extra Small.03

Oriental
Owner-designed
Islington, London, 2000

This garden was created when the owners of the townhouse converted the building at the back of their land into a sitting room with a bedroom above. The garden, which was already small, suddenly became even smaller.

The new sitting room extended outwards and ate away at the back of the space. A covered walkway was built to link the house to the new rooms and the garden space was cut back even further. What was left was a tiny, sunken area surrounded on all sides by walls. The owners, one of whom designed the garden, were happy to compromise on its size: 'The garden had to be big enough to enjoy, but given the weather in the UK, we opted for increased indoor space.'

The tiny space that was left could have been a cause for despair. But what the owners have created is a lovely, leafy hideaway courtyard, which at night comes alive with lighting. The key here was having a theme.

However, 'theme' might be the wrong word. Themed gardens encourage images of gnomes and Disneyland – what this garden has is an idea, a character, and the owners have kept this in mind throughout the design: 'We didn't want anything fake – it's a matter of applying touches to add flavour, to create a look.' The 'look' is Eastern exotic, with touches from Indonesia and Morocco, and a large dose of the owners' own style. Because they have been so true to their original concept, they have created a complete ambience in their garden, rather than a pastiche.

Designer's tip If you can work out a theme, a definite look or character you want from your garden, it can help with every decision along the way – from how to divide up the space, to which plants to use, to colour selection and choice of furniture.

Inside, the house is full of furniture from the Far East and pieces found in salvage yards. One of the owners is a furniture designer, and has a great eye for what will work and for pulling it together. Outside, the same ideas have been carried through into the garden. An enormous mirror covers one wall, and interesting pieces of sculpture hide in the greenery. The size of these pieces may be surprising, but they fit with the large leaves of the jungle planting. Like remnants of a lost world of giants, they add an element of the bizarre to the garden. The sculptures were designed by the owner and his friend. They are created from polystyrene, made into a mould, with the final sculpture coated in a mix of limestone powder giving the appearance of real stone.

Designer's tip Objects that challenge the scale of a space, especially if stumbled upon in the garden, are great fun. Fallen columns, industrial salvage or items from agricultural auctions can all be used to make sculpture. Lit at night, their forms can take on a completely different air.

At the other end of the scale from these oversized objects, the small details in the garden also carry on the theme. For example, inset into the paving, small mosaic pieces add interest to Chinese slate squares.

The lights in this garden complete the look. During the day they provide beautiful decoration, and at night the garden is alive with colour. The main light was adapted from a candleholder. The owner of the garden used opaque

DESIGN BRIEF
• A good view, day and night
• Somewhere to sit
• To act as extension of house

FEATURES
• Raised bed for shrubs
• Architectural sculpture
• Coloured-glass light fittings

Perspex to line the inside of the holder to hide his newly fitted light bulb, and the whole thing was fixed to a pole hanging over the garden. The other two lights have coloured-glass beads and a pattern of swirling holes that throw colour over the walls at night. In amongst the foliage, and uplighting the statuary, spotlights give dots of colour.

The colours also help the garden to connect to the inside. Deep, rich reds, bright yellows and dark greens predominate, and the same earthy colours are found indoors. These are exotic colours, but not alien to the light here. Where Grecian blues that look so good under white-hot Mediterranean light do not transfer, earthy tones work well with the duller light in the UK.

On a practical note, the planting, lush though it is, has been pretty much confined to one wall. This leaves maximum space for play and sitting. If the planting carried on around the other sides of the garden, the space would have felt too overgrown and light into the house would have

been curtailed. The plants have been chosen to provide year-round greenery. The camellia and fatsia have beautiful glossy green leaves and will survive in the darkest corner, while above them, reaching for the light, is flannel bush (*Fremontodendron*), a semi-hardy wall shrub that produces yellow flowers in spring and autumn. The chusan palm (*Trachycarpus fortunei*) gives a spiky feel to the lower planting.

This garden shows what you can do without spending huge amounts of money and without vast amounts of garden. With a clear idea of the feel they were trying to achieve, the owners have created an outside space that fits their needs and personalities and has its own distinct character, which derives directly from the interior of the house to complete the picture.

ABOVE: Oversized statuary (made by the owner) gives the garden a theatrical element.

LEFT: Lights are important to this tiny courtyard, and make it more inviting at night.

Plants for shady areas

A courtyard, almost by definition, is shady much of the time, and especially so here in the heart of the city where it is surrounded by tall buildings. But, if you go with the conditions and do not try to fight them, it is possible to have some wonderful planting.

The most enjoyable garden I ever had was a tiny north-facing patio that I filled to breaking point with plants. It had no soil, so everything was in containers that I moved around as things developed to make an ever-changing scene. I do not think there is a name for this type of mobile gardening, but it is very enjoyable and, because the garden was so small, I knew every last inch of it. I would watch as things came on ready to take centre stage and know what to move away. This intimate knowledge is something that, on a larger scale, is pretty much impossible.

So if you have a small courtyard, count your blessings – at least it is manageable. The following shady-areas planting list starts with the tall structural plants and also includes suggestions for middle- and lower-layer plants for seasonal interest.

BELOW: Tiny shady courtyards can be transformed into dramatic places with large-leaved plants and huge sculptures lit from below.

Castor oil plant (*Fatsia japonica*)
Evergreen bushy shrub with large glossy leaves.

Tree ivy (x *Fatshedera lizei*)
Fatsia's climbing relative. It will need tying in to get up to a good height.

Mexican orange blossom (*Choisya ternate*)
A scented yet quite thuggish plant that can outgrow a small garden, but if you want something to fill a space, this is it.

Sweet box (*Sarcococca hookeriana* var. *digyna*)
This is a 'must have' for a shady courtyard. Most of the year you will not even know it is there, but in late winter the place will be filled with the sweet scent of its flowers.

Japanese anemone 'September' (*Anemone* x *hybrida* 'September Charm')
These late summer flowers give dots of white that work brilliantly in low, shady light.

Armenian cranesbill (*Geranium psilostemon*)
A monster of a geranium with quite outrageous cerise flowers in mid-summer.

Lady's mantle (*Alchemilla mollis*)
A great low grower for the front of the border, with beautiful leaves and yellow-green flowers.

Ajuga reptans 'Multicolor'
Another one for the front, which fits well with alchemilla, this has dark-purple leaves with pink and white markings.

Ivy-leaved cyclamen (*Cyclamen hederifolium*)
The leaves on this plant would be enough to recommend it, as they have beautiful silvery patterns, but in autumn it also has pink flowers.

Scaly male fern (*Dryopteris affinis*)
This fern, with yellow leaves when young, maturing to rich green, is wonderful in dry shade.

Extra Small.04

45-Degree
Philip Nash
Middlesex, 2003

The roof space here had to be a garden. Not a terrace. Not a balcony. Designer Philip Nash's aim was to 'create a garden that could have been on the ground, and lift it on to the roof'.

This said, it is not just a back garden on high – there is plenty in this space that cleverly takes into account the problems of roof gardens and at the same time makes the most of the views.

The garden is a textbook example of a design at 45 degrees. From the entrance, a path leads off diagonally across the space, and the beds and seating areas work off from this main angle.

The diagonal design has allowed two distinct seating areas to be created: one with a freestanding table and chairs, the other with built-in seats. Here, another advantage of the angled design becomes apparent. The inbuilt seats face out to the sides, to the surrounding views, rather than looking straight back at the entrance to the garden.

Designer's tip Designs at 45 degrees immediately give a dynamic to what might be a fairly straightforward division of the space. Interesting angles and hidden areas are created, and the eye is taken to the sides rather than drawn directly to the end of the garden.

Hidden underneath the seats is lighting and speakers for a sound system, which is controlled from inside the house. The speakers are waterproof and intended for outdoor use. However, putting them under the seats means the sound is not lost to the air.

At the centre of the garden is a water feature designed and built by Philip Nash. Water flows up through the triangular column and over the top. A light inside shines through the cut-out design on the side and travels up to catch the lip of water as it flows over the top. Within the garden, the eye is drawn to the water feature by metal grating running straight to it from the entrance. 'When you enter the garden,' says Philip, 'you get the impression of water coming towards you underneath the grating.' At the base of the water feature is a shallow pond with two cages of horsetails (*Equisetum*) and, underneath these at the base, dark pebbles line the pond.

Designer's tip The darker the pond, the better the reflections will be. The dark pebbles here help to reflect the sky, and also cover the lining on the bottom.

Around the built-in seating area and the pond are raised beds with lush, architectural planting. Yuccas and bamboos give height and the feeling of enclosure that is so important in creating the feel of this garden. Under these are some quite tender plants, like bottlebrush (*Callistemon subulatus*) and oleander. At the lowest level, black grass (*Ophiopogon planiscapus* 'Nigrescens') and sedums form the under-planting. The planting is used for form and texture rather than for flowers, and the angular patterns of many of the plants give strong shapes to compete with the urban skyline.

Along one side of the garden, existing storage boxes have been retained, but finished to match the raised beds with the same textured rubberoid paint and aluminium edging.

The immediate impression here is of a well-designed, small-space garden. However, to find the really clever bits

---

DESIGN BRIEF
- A garden in the sky
- Two sitting areas
- Shelter from wind

FEATURES
- Raised beds
- Water feature
- Metal floor grille

of this design, it is necessary to go behind the scenes a little.

Weight is one of the most important issues with roof gardens. A structural engineer advised on the maximum weights that could be used here, and also identified the strongest points of the roof that could take more load. The design and planting was based around this. To keep the weight down, the raised beds are made of outdoor marine ply with a support frame. They are lightweight, but just robust enough, and the textured paint and aluminium edgings were used to give them a much more substantial look. Inside the raised beds, polystyrene has been used to keep down the need for heavy soil, but for bigger plants the depth of soil has been increased around their roots. The planters are lined with fibreglass and a geotextile membrane – the former to increase the longevity of the ply, the latter to help with drainage.

Surprisingly for a roof garden, this one is not flat. Low steps have been incorporated into the design to help define different areas and give another dimension of interest. The steps also raise up the decking so that the pond sits flush with 'ground' level and there is space underneath for electrical cables for lights and the sound system.

Designer's tip This is an excellent use of decking. Raising the floor level up by a few inches would have been a nightmare with stone, but comes naturally to decking. Decking is also a relatively light material, so works well on roof gardens.

This is a wonderful example of a garden that has to work together as a whole; the entire structure is held together from below with tensioned wire.

The garden also accommodates the less technical elements of roof gardens – the competing demands of retaining the surrounding views and the need for privacy and shelter. It is necessary to feel a little enclosed to feel comfortable, and this is achieved here by placing the highest raised bed, containing the tallest planting of golden bamboos (*Phyllostachys aurea*) and Spanish dagger (*Yucca gloriosa*) behind the inbuilt seating area. These plants also help to cut down the prevailing winds. But there is no point having a roof garden if the views are blocked. To resolve this, Philip has carefully left open the view to the river and across the roof tops, and where he has put in screening it has been designed to reflect the rooftop patterns of the surrounding buildings.

There is nothing delicate or unsure about this garden. The planting is architectural and sturdy enough to withstand the elements. The lines of the garden are also clear and strong. And the technical design is accomplished. The demands of making a garden and making it work are very difficult in circumstances like these, but there is a real synergy here between the practical, technical demands of the site and the need for an aesthetically pleasing garden. On top of this, Philip Nash has managed to create an atmosphere, rather than just a decorated space; it is, most definitely, a garden.

BELOW LEFT: The perfectly horizontal top encourages the water to flow in a clean line over the lip of the water feature.

BELOW MIDDLE: Metal grating forms a 'path' running diagonally from the water feature to the entrance.

BELOW RIGHT: Horsetails (*Equisetum*) are planted in wire cages to stop their invasive habits.

ABOVE: Substantial plants form a windbreak around the main seating area.

Roof gardens

There are worse places to create a garden, but on top of a roof has to be fairly high up the list. Drying winds, lack of shade, weight restrictions and no soil – it is a wonder anyone tries at all. But since the Hanging Gardens of Babylon, roof gardens have proved that they can be magical spaces. The design possibilities are limitless, but there are some basic things to consider:

- Regulations may have an impact on what you want to do. Building regulations stipulate the type of barrier that needs to be placed around the garden, and also what you use on the floor. It is worth checking to see if you need planning permission as well.
- If you have a roof that might be turned into a garden, the first thing to do is to get in an architect or structural engineer to talk about weight and whether your roof is strong enough to hold plants, soil, floor material and people.
- Apart from weight restrictions, the potential of strong winds also needs to be taken into

consideration. Trellises need to be attached securely, and plants anchored in. It is also worth finding out where the prevailing wind comes from, and forming a screen to make the space more usable.

Designer's tip Strangely, solid screens are not ideal. In any situation where you are trying to cut down wind, a semi-permeable screen will work best. You want to slow the wind, not stop it. Stopping it will force it up and over the top and, inevitably, back down again.

- Whether you want a lush or minimalist garden, if you have plants you will have to use containers. To create atmosphere with dense planting, raised beds will probably work best, but are heavier and more expensive than smaller containers and pots, which although easier to put in, do dry out more quickly and can get blown over.
- Whatever type of containers you use, the plants will need a lot of water. Containers with limited soil will hold less water than the ground. Add to this the drying

effects of the wind and an irrigation system begins to look like a worthwhile labour-saver. Whether you water by hand or automatically, make sure excess water can drain away, and safely, off the roof.

- As in this garden, it is a good idea to save on weight by using polystyrene or perlite instead of soil at the bottom of the containers. A peat substitute is lighter than ordinary loam-based compost.
- If you are using raised beds, make sure the roots of plants are contained well within the beds and, if you have smaller containers, check occasionally to make sure the roots have not worked their way out and into the roof.
- Roof gardens have enormous benefits for both users and the environment. They create green spaces in urban environments, help to remove carbon dioxide, insulate the building below, and can be enormous fun.

Extra Small.05

Green and White

Owner designed
Bow, London, 2003

People think it is impossible to do minimalist if you have children. Well, not if you have a wall. The wall here almost spans the width of the garden and provides both a focal point and a place to put all of those inevitable bits of plastic that small children accumulate.

This is a brilliant and beautifully proportioned garden, all the more amazing as it was designed by the owner, who has no formal training in garden design. He knew the look he wanted to create before he started: 'I wanted something minimalist, but also green.' What he has achieved is a deceptively simple design, yet one that works hard and looks striking.

The layout is quite straightforward – divided into three areas. The owner wanted to create 'three additional rooms – a dining room, a garden and a hideaway'. The 'dining room' just outside the house is decked and contains a sitting area, shaded by a sail sunshade. Low white walls enclose this area, separating it from the rest of the garden. The gap in the walls creates an entrance to the garden and the feeling of entering another space.

The 'garden' area is a rectangle of lawn surrounded by off-white Caliza Capri polished limestone squares. These are laid formally and their light colour immediately gives the area a clean and modern feel. Along the sides are box bushes (*Buxus sempervirens*) clipped into balls, and behind these are raised beds of rendered stone, painted white to carry on, and reinforce, the lines of the limestone. The perimeter walls to either side are covered in ivy, which is maintained vigorously to keep it looking neat.

At the rear of the lawn is the wall. Rather than just a plain wall, a slit has been created down the middle to give interest. Not only does this gap give a vertical line and central point to the symmetry of the garden, it also has an interesting purpose. It is narrower at the back than the front, so you cannot see into the rear from the main part of the garden. But from behind you have a wide view of what is going on in the rest of the garden.

From this gap, a water rill runs into the grass: 'We painted the insides of the slit black so that it looks like the water might be running from the top of the wall down into the rill.' This water feature is safe in a way I have never seen before, as the narrow rill means that they cannot get their faces in it.

The wall is perfectly proportioned for the garden and creates a hidden area behind for storing toys. It also acts as a screen on which to show films at night, and is a great backdrop for fireworks. As if this wasn't enough, behind the wall the owners have created a secluded, inbuilt seating area. Surrounded by bamboos, it is totally hidden from the house and neighbours and makes a wonderfully quiet place to sit or to play.

This simple arrangement of three areas works very well, but it is the proportions that make the garden beautiful. The wall is just the right height to hold the area without dominating it, and the limestone path and grass work together, neither taking over, both complementing the space.

Designer's tip Proportions are difficult to get right in any design. You can go by eye or use the proportions of the house as a guide. Or you can use thirds, as has been done here. However you go about it, it is wise to mark out the areas on the ground before you start and live with them for a while to make sure the divisions feel right.

DESIGN BRIEF
- Create three rooms
- Minimalist
- Limited colour palette

FEATURES
- White wall
- Rill running into lawn
- Limestone paving

The planting also completes the limited colour palette of white, black and green, with touches of silver from accessories. White is used for lines and uprights. Viewing the garden from the house, it is the whites that jump out to create a bold, symmetrical pattern, leading the eye towards the vanishing point.

Black has been used for the seating areas. The deck next to the house has been painted black to separate it visually from the rest of the garden and to create a contrast with the white of the limestone. And around the back of the wall, the inbuilt seating is black against a white retaining wall.

Silver has been used sparingly. The tree ferns are set in round silver tubs. On the wall in the 'dining room' is a silver wreath, and next to this is a silver-tube water feature that is visible from the kitchen window.

The whole design is brought together and reinforced by the limited planting scheme. Imagine this same design, but with cottagey planting around. It would be a totally different garden. As it is, the controlled minimalism of the design has been carried through with a controlled, minimalist plant list. All the plants are architectural and structured, and unrelentingly green. Ivy on the walls, box bushes clipped into tight ball shapes, cloud pruned holly (*Ilex crenata*), broad-leaved bamboos (*Sasa palmata*) and tree ferns (*Dicksonia antarctica*). With the exception of the tree ferns, all are evergreen, so the garden will look as wonderful in winter as in summer. A limited planting like this not only looks good, it makes a garden easier to look after. Maintenance is much simpler if there are only a few different plants to tend to.

Designer's tip Painted decking is wonderful for effect, but fairly high maintenance. For example, this deck is recoated twice a year to keep it spotless.

This garden is a perfect fusion of the needs of adults and children. The children, even in winter, can run around, play outside and hide behind the wall. They can put their hands in the running water but be quite safe. And the adults have a beautiful space to enjoy – for eating out, for entertaining and for watching films.

ABOVE: Behind the wall is a secluded sitting area, surrounded by bamboo and with a stylish, inbuilt seat.

BELOW: The wonderful symmetry of the garden creates a precise, yet restful, picture.

ABOVE: Separated by a low wall, the dining area is the first of the garden's three areas.

Designing your own garden

The owner of this garden designed it himself, and despite no training or experience has produced an accomplished design. If you want to design your own garden, there is a very logical, step-by-step process for doing so, based on the constraints and opportunities the garden presents, and on how you want to use it:

• First you need to do a scale drawing. Measure up the garden and draw it, to scale, on paper. For a small- to medium-size garden, 2 centimetres for each metre (about 0.2 inches for each foot) will usually do. Mark on the drawing anything that is going to impinge on the design – a tree you cannot remove, a view you want to hide, entrances and exits. You can see immediately that, if tackling the design of your garden yourself, a smaller garden will be much less of a challenge.

• It is best to have a clear idea of the look you want to achieve before you begin. This helps to narrow down the possibilities. The owner here took inspiration from the Hempel Hotel in London, which has a lawn defined by light-coloured paving with contemporary planting around the sides. If you can find inspiration from a single photograph or particular garden, the design will come more easily and be more uniform.

• Consider how you want to use the garden as this, too, will narrow down how you divide up the space. Here the owner knew he wanted three areas, and the design flowed from there.

• I find that it is best not to sit in the garden or look at it when you are designing, as it is all too easy to be distracted by what is already there. Go inside with just the scale drawing and your inspiration.

• Unless you are very keen on DIY, once you have got the design

outline it is probably worth calling on contractors to build the garden. The contractors for this garden were Outerspace, who worked with the client to bring his ideas to life. Good contractors will not just implement the plan – they will improve upon it.

• If you do get stuck, a garden designer can help enormously. Many garden designers will come along for a one-off consultation to talk through any problems you are having or to set you off in the right direction. Most have websites that you can check out to see whether their style fits with your ideas.

S

Small

S Introduction

A little more room creates greater flexibility – for example, with regard to where the seating area should go – and may also mean a hidden swing or small pool can be accommodated. Movement around the garden also becomes an issue, as areas can be screened off to create separate 'rooms'.

Division of the space is a core principle of garden design. If you can divide up an area, you can create more interest, excitement and purpose by using architecture, structure and proportions to form naturally harmonious spaces that work within the garden and for how it will be used.

However, the divisions that form these spaces do not need to be 'real' – they can be implied. In some of the gardens in this section, the divides are just low walls, yet still create a feeling of entering a totally different space. For example, in the Wisteria and Glass garden a seating area is divided off by a low wall with wooden uprights. Entering the space feels like stepping into a separate room, but it is all but open to the rest of the garden. Different areas are instantly attractive places for children. Here, the corner seat provides a quiet spot for the girls to sit. In the Mediterranean Modern garden, the area under the tree at the rear is a magnet for children to explore and play.

Despite this increased scope for division and interest, small gardens still require a strong structure, and those that work best have tight designs. As with very small gardens, there is still no room for dead corners or informal areas – every part needs to be used and included within the overall design.

A bit more space also means more scope to experiment with planting. Beds can be larger, and each square inch of soil does not come under the same degree

BELOW: In slightly larger spaces, there is more scope to include different types of water features and sitting areas. This one beautifully combines both bench and water.

ABOVE: Hard landscaping, rather than lawn, works very well in a small space.

BELOW: A raised bed above the water feature makes the most of a limited space.

of scrutiny. In the Mediterranean Modern garden, the owners have sacrificed a lawn so that they can have beds large enough to include a greater variety of plants that maintain continually changing interest throughout the seasons.

Lawns tend to dominate small gardens and to dictate the design; they are usually front and centre, and the rest of the design needs to work around them. In little spaces, limitations like these may be unbearable. In addition, storing a lawnmower can be an effort, grass can be difficult to walk across during the winter and, for small areas, the cost of hard landscaping instead of lawn is not going to be too expensive. Given all of this, most people decide against lawns for small areas.

One of the challenges when designing a small garden is to make it appear bigger and lighter. There are a number of ways to achieve this:

- **Unifying walls** If walls are harmonious, they blend into the background. The easiest way to achieve this is to use the same trellis around the walls, or by rendering and painting their internal surfaces.
- **Planting on walls** The walls in a small garden may be the largest single area in the garden and using them for planting will increase the interest of the garden. In the Sophisticated Rooms garden, a single type of climber, star jasmine (*Trachelospermum jasminoides*), has been used all along the top half of the garden to give colour and scent, and to unify the look.
- **Mirrors** Mirrors work in two ways: they bounce light around and can also give the illusion of a larger garden. In the Wisteria and Glass garden, mirrors are half hidden on the rear wall to give the impression of windows.
- **Raised beds** Raised beds really come into their own in smaller gardens. There is enough ground space to accommodate them, and they help to define areas and can create inbuilt seating.
- **Linking inside and out** A popular way of increasing the apparent size of a small garden is to link the house and garden. Many of the garden designs in this book, both small and large, are the result of extensions to the rears of houses. These extensions, with their abundant use of glass and huge doors, help enormously in blurring the boundaries between inside and out. Using similar materials on the floors, and a unified sense of design for both interior and exterior, also helps create a single, flowing space.

Small.01

Wisteria and Glass

Claire Mee
Fulham, London, 2003

The design for this small city garden has taken on board all of the points of the design brief and has resulted in a garden that is both beautiful and easy to live with. The designer, Claire Mee, has created a very soft garden with few hard edges, and with an air of the countryside about it. Hard lines are used sparingly to give structure and balance to what could have been just a mass of planting. A central lawn butts up to the house, with planting along each side.

The garden's main solid outline is the low wall protecting a shaded seating area to the rear. The wall acts as a visual divide and, from within the seating area, helps to create the feeling of being in a separate space. It also provides an entrance to the seating area over to one side of the garden. The divide is continued upwards with wooden uprights entwined with wisteria. However, overhead, wires instead of wood are used across the top to let in light and stop the structure being, as the designer says, 'too dark, heavy and woody'. The wires are 3-millimetre (0.1-inch) stainless steel bought from a local chandler.

The overhead wires help train the climbing wisteria (*Wisteria sinensis*) and have beautiful blue candleholders hanging from them. Also in this space is a large storage area, tucked away under an inbuilt seat, and large enough to house the lawn mower and other garden implements. The seat provides a hideaway for the two children, a place to sit, play or read. Along the rear fence are half-concealed mirrors that bounce the light around and look like windows, looking out through the rear boundary.

Scent is important in this semi-enclosed area. 'The

Designer's tip If you are putting mirrors on a wall, the trick is to make sure the edges are hidden. In this garden they are hidden with battens and star jasmine, a climber that is semi-hardy so will survive in a sheltered spot like this, giving lovely scented white flowers in the summer.

scents will be much stronger here than out in the open, so we didn't use too many competing flavours, or it would be overpowering,' says Claire. Wisteria, star jasmin (*Trachelospermum jasminoides*) and lavender (*Lavandula angustifolia* 'Hidcote') provide the limited palette of summer scents.

The colour theme of the plants is white, purple, grey and pink. The grey is provided by the leaves of the lavenders, olives (*Olea europaea*), rosemary (*Rosmarinus officinalis*) and catmint (*Nepeta* 'Six Hills Giant'). The predominant colour of the flowers is purple, with wisteria, ceanothus and, later in the year, the lavenders. In amongst these are white campanulas (*Campanula persicifolia* var. *alba*), a variety of roses and, next to the house, a splash of vivid pink is provided by a row of terracotta pots planted up with bright pink geraniums.

Over to one side is a swing for the two girls to play on. Made from natural materials, it blends in with the surrounding planting, seemingly anchored in it. On the floor are bark chippings that, again, being natural do not jar with the surroundings. The swing is on the north-facing shady side of the garden. It is important to provide shade in areas where children may be playing for hours at a time to avoid sunburn. On the south-facing side is a sunny bench – the 'seat in the sun' from the brief – for adults. And around the garden, small, cordoned fruit trees give another dimension

DESIGN FEATURE
- Something for the children, but not a 'children's garden'
- Somewhere to eat outside in the shade
- A seat in the sun
- Storage
- A soft garden, full of flowers, to contrast with the very modern house extension

FEATURES
- Seating area with wooden uprights and wires across the top
- Hidden swing
- Mirrors on the rear fence
- Cobbles for transition from house to lawn

to the planting, providing an autumn harvest as well as a spring blossom.

There is no planting right next to the house. The huge glass wall opens straight out on to lawn with only a narrow line of cobbles on the ground as a buffer; planting along here would interfere with the wall-to-ceiling, side-to-side glass. The cobbles, running alongside the house, are an important detail; without them it would be difficult to mow the grass where it meets the house.

Around the boundaries of the garden the trelliswork has been replaced and topped off with battens. Previously there were five different types of fencing around the garden. According to the designer: 'You need to impose order, but don't want to block anyone's light.' The battening gives a unified feel to the whole garden and looks more contemporary than plain trellis.

What has been created here is a very pretty, feminine garden that is balanced rather than symmetrical. The

dining area to the rear, with its dappled shade and views back to the house, mirrors the large kitchen/dining room inside the house. It is a garden that blossoms into life in the summer, with campanulas, roses and ceanothus, but it also has an underlying structure that anchors this abundance in the warmer months and provides interest in the winter. Carefully positioned evergreen box bushes (*Buxus sempervirens*) clipped into ball shapes, the evergreen olives and the hard landscaping give it life even in the depths of winter.

ABOVE: The new extension to the house backs on to the garden, with an uninterrupted glass wall blurring the boundary between inside and out.

RIGHT: Star jasmine (*Trachelospermum jasminoides*) growing over mirrors adds to the illusion that they are windows, looking out to the rear of the garden.

OPPOSITE: Made from wood, the swing blends in with the garden, but is still great fun for the children.

ABOVE: In the dining area, an inbuilt seat doubles up as storage space and provides a shady, sheltered place to sit.

BELOW: At the rear of the garden, a low wall and wooden uprights give the dining area a feeling of being separate, yet not cut off, from the rest of the garden.

ABOVE: Cobbles alongside the house separate it from the lawn so the grass can be cut easily, but do not interfere with the view from the huge glass window at the rear.

Designing a small city-garden

Claire Mee has been designing gardens in London for many years and has met, and overcome, most of the problems they can present. She suggests the following guidelines for creating the perfect small city-garden:

Dividing up the garden
'People think that sectioning off areas will make the garden look smaller, but it doesn't. If you can't see the whole garden at once, it will make it appear larger and give so much more interest.' In this garden, the extra 'room' at the rear obscures the boundary and makes the whole seem bigger.

Boundaries
City gardens tend to inherit lots of different boundary fences and walls: 'It's like having a living room with different wallpaper on each wall – you need to make it more cohesive.' Claire uses battening and trelliswork to unify the boundaries, instantly creating a cleaner look to the garden.

Light
Lack of light is often a problem in small gardens, making them appear dark and dingy. Bare red brick is a particularly bad offender, as it sucks up light. Using light-coloured materials for trelliswork, painting walls and using render that can then be painted a light

colour can all help to bounce around what light there is. 'You can also try using mirrors, as we have here, to increase light levels in small spaces,' says Claire.

Materials
'In a small space it's often possible to use really good materials, as the cost won't be so prohibitive if there aren't too many square metres to fund. We want our gardens to look as good in 10 years' time as they did the day they went in, and more expensive materials will achieve that.' Natural materials are often the best, and wear extremely well. Claire suggests Indian sandstone as a good, natural and reasonably priced paving.

Seating areas
Most gardens need a place to sit, and Claire tries to position the seating area away from the house. 'If the seating area is next to the house, the rest of the garden can become neglected, but with a sitting area at the rear of the garden you have to make the journey through the garden. And when you're sitting there looking back through planting and greenery to the house, it feels like you're in the country.'

Specimen plants
Claire often uses large specimen plants. The wisterias and the olives in this garden were bought large. 'My clients often want an instant effect,

and in a city garden you can get that by putting in a few large plants, which can make all the difference in a small space.'

Planting
Planting of all sorts brings a garden to life: 'As soon as we've planted up a garden, you can hear the buzz of insects, and once you've got insects you'll get birds.' Claire is particularly keen on planting small fruit trees in city gardens so that children can see how they develop from blossom, enjoy eating the produce and learn, as Claire says, 'that fruit doesn't just come from supermarkets'.

Small.02

Exotic Heat Island
Karen Fitzsimon
Highbury, London, 2003–05

This is a great garden (and house) to refer to if you are tight on space and want to make the most of it. The story of the garden here starts with the house; more room was needed inside, but its Grade II listing meant that any changes had to be in keeping with the original building. Even more of a constraint was the lack of space in this highly built-up corner of London. The ingenious solution was to build an extension to the rear and side of the house. Infilling the area to the side of the house gave space for storage and a corridor on the ground floor, and an extended bedroom above.

The extension was the impetus for changing the garden, and landscape architect Karen Fitzsimon used the same ingenuity in the limited space outside. The brief was for a garden the two boys (ages six and nine) could play in, but also one in which the adults could 'indulge their love of plants'. However, before any designs could be considered, the huge problem of creating a new garden needed to be overcome.

Concrete on the ground, up to a metre (3.2 feet) thick, could not be removed. And there was no soil for plants for the adults, or for grass for the children. Many designers at this point would have taken the easy route and suggested hard landscaping and containers. However, roof-garden technology has enabled a 'proper' garden to be established.

The lawn was made possible by using a thin layer of soil with a special water-dispensing material underneath, so that the water does not pool on the concrete. Geovoid 30, by Greenfix, is a magical material that moves excess water away, but also retains a certain amount, to prevent waterlogging when it rains and drying out in the summer. In effect, this membrane replicates the action of soil. For the planting around the lawn, which required deeper soil, the solution was to go up, using raised beds.

The initial constraints of the space were, in the end, turned into advantages. The walls around the raised beds mean that the delicate plants are less likely to be damaged by the boys playing football. And the retaining walls also provide lots of space-saving seating for parties and family get-togethers. The raised beds give wonderful structure to the garden, and the unusual plants can be seen much better in their elevated positions.

So the rear garden is a simple, central lawn surrounded by raised beds. But this is only the beginning of the story. Every part of this garden has been thought about and used to great effect. A particularly good example of this is the specially designed garden room in the far corner, built as a den for the children but which will outlast their needs and become, in time, a studio for adults.

Designer's tip Children grow up and their needs change. It is worth calculating how much use they are going to get out of anything you put in the garden for them. The den in this garden was a large investment, but worth it because it is not just for the children. It will, as Karen Fitzsimon says, 'hold its own in the garden as a feature once the kids have moved on from it'.

The den, with heating and lighting, is set into the corner at an angle, its two front sides opening up completely to the garden. It was made by the English

---

DESIGN BRIEF
• Interesting plants
• Play areas for children
• Lawn

FEATURES
• Den for children
• Raised beds
• Bicycle shelter

LEFT TO RIGHT: The beautiful, bespoke bike shed fits in perfectly with the garden; Tucked away in the corner of the garden is a den, built with both children and adults in mind; Down the side of the house, a light and airy storage space leads through to a leafy courtyard.

Garden Carpentry Company, which specialises in bespoke, interesting designs. What is immediately noticeable is that there is no gap for getting into the den in the low wall that goes around the garden. For aesthetic reasons, this is to keep the line of the wall going round the garden, but, most importantly, it was designed this way to increase the sense of fun and adventure for the children as they enter. When the den is a pirate ship, they can stand on the wall to keep lookout across the seas.

Down from the building and tucked away in a corner is a raised pool. It is small, but almost as soon as it was put in it began attracting wildlife and, however tiny, it also gives the opportunity for pond plants in this small garden.

And plants are to a large extent what this garden is about. The owners and designer have exploited the warmth of this sheltered city garden to try out non-hardy plants that would not survive elsewhere. More tender plants have been mixed in with hardy ones to create an interesting combination of flowers and structure. However, the overall effect is exotic. Agaves (*Agave americana*), bananas (*Musa basjoo*), palms and tree ferns (*Dicksonia Antarctica*) give structure and architecture to the planting, while agapanthus (*Agapanthus africanus*) and delicate grasses like festuca (*Festuca glauca* 'Elijah Blue') form an understorey to the jungle.

From above, the view of the garden is striking, its curving wall giving a beautiful strong line. But this is not a symmetrical garden; the curve of the wall is quite freeform, which though not obvious from the ground, from above makes the garden look much less clinical and more organic.

Designer's tip In any garden, but especially in a small garden next to a tall townhouse, one of the most important views will be from above. Here, a strong, clearly defined design will be much more striking. In this garden, says Karen, even some of the plants have been chosen with this in mind. 'Plants like the tree fern and the echiums (*Echium pininana*) in particular look fantastic from above.'

The storage for the garden is tucked away in the side extension to the house and, through this extension, towards the front of the house, is another area of the garden – a tiny courtyard. Again, raised beds have been used for plants and seating, and the area, while utilitarian, has been created with an eye for beauty. A bike shelter is not normally something remarkable. But this one is. It seems the English Garden Carpentry Company does more than just carpentry; it also designed and made this wonderful shelter for the site. Formed from stainless steel with a laminated roof covered in lead, the details are wonderful and encapsulate this quirky, bespoke garden.

This was a very tricky garden to design, with many demands being put on a very small space and, of course, the huge drawback of the lack of soil. But rather than going for the easy route, the designer and owners have taken the time to make a unique garden, with detailing and features that could so easily have been missed out, but would have been missed. The garden has an organic feel that, along with the exotic planting, makes it a very personal creation.

LEFT TO RIGHT: Agapanthus (*Agapanthus africanus*), banana (*Musa basjoo*) and montbretia (*Crocosmia* 'Lucifer').

Exotic heat islands

This is the name Angus White, from Architectural Plants, gives to the potential of gardens in large cities. He comes up with some startling statistics. The minimum temperature in London in winter is comparable to the south coast of France. Of course, it is hotter in the summer in France, but it is this minimum temperature that is important for plants' survival and happiness. On one of the coldest nights in recent history, in 1991, Angus recorded a temperature of −17°C in West Sussex. In London on the same night, the minimum was −4°C, an enormous 13°C difference. This 'heat island' effect is huge, and its benefits are little exploited.

In any city area, the buildings and roads will absorb heat during the day and release it at night. Add to this central heating, cars and people and you have an enormous amount of heat being generated and, the larger the city, the more extreme this will be.

Angus has understandable caveats about suggesting going for very tender plants. If there is one thing we can predict about the British weather, it is that it is unpredictable. But if you want to try something different, a whole new world of less hardy plants opens up. These are architectural, unusual and beautiful, and most are evergreen:

Oven's wattle (*Acacia pravissima*)
A spreading, small evergreen tree with bright yellow flowers early spring.

Yucca-leaved beschorneria (*Beschorneria yuccoides*)
This looks like a yucca, but has red flower spikes early in the year.

Silver Spear (*Astelia chathamica*)
Silvery-blue sword-shaped leaves.

Callistemon subulatus
An evergreen shrub with red 'bottlebrush' flowers in summer.

Umbrella plant (*Cyperus alternifolius*)
A short papyrus with a distinctive leaf arrangement.

Giant viper's bugloss (*Echium pininana*)
This is a short-lived plant, but it produces amazing 2.4-metre-high (8-foot-high) flowers.

Fascicularia pitcairniifolia
A relative of the pineapple with extraordinary red and blue flowers.

Kahili ginger (*Hedychium gardnerianum*)
A ginger lily with fragrant yellow flowers.

Mitre flower (*Mitraria coccinea*)
An evergreen climber with exotic red flowers in late spring.

Chinese rice-paper plant (*Tetrapanax papyrifer*)
An evergreen with huge leaves and white flowers in summer followed by black berries in the autumn.

Small.03

Sophisticated Rooms
Philip Nash
Clapham, London, 2004

Gardens on slopes are always a little troublesome; small gardens on slopes are just plain difficult. And those that slope down, away from the house, are usually the most difficult of all. Decking platforms that stretch out above the garden are often the best solution in cases like this, and avoid trying to build up the land to meet the house.

The good news here is that the garden slopes up from the house, so it was not necessary to create flat spaces out of thin air. But it is so small that any changes in level needed to take into account the levels of the land in the neighbours' gardens on both sides. To create a usable flat space outside the house, the land has been taken back. Retaining walls were necessary on each side to hold up the existing levels of the neighbouring gardens. And at the rear of the patio area directly outside the house, the wall needed to be tall and substantial enough to hold back the rest of the garden.

With a larger garden it is possible to create a flat area within, without affecting the boundaries. You might even get away with grading off the land in all directions without the need for retaining walls. But in small gardens you inevitably run out of space to create slopes.

And space is very tight in this garden. The brief given to the designer, Philip Nash, was not only to make a usable area for sitting and eating, but also to create a green jungle feeling and room outside for work and play. Quite a lot to fit into a small area.

The sitting area at the lowest level has retaining walls on three sides, but these have been used to great effect to create a real feeling of an outside room. The walls have been rendered and painted in a single colour to enclose a beautiful modern courtyard. Above the walls, horizontal trelliswork finishes off the look.

Designer's tip The render here is called Monocouche, and is very easy to use. Getting a smooth surface is straightforward; just pile it on the wall and then scrape it down with a special tool. The resulting surface is uniformly textured.

The walls, built out of necessity, have been turned to good use in the overall design and also used for features within the design. Along the rear of the sitting area, the retaining wall holds a water feature from which water drops down into a rill that runs right across the garden.

The water feature is quite complex, with a central pool of water held in a stainless-steel trough. The sides of the trough are perfectly horizontal to allow a film of water to fall over it in all directions. The water falls into a lower trough that, in turn, lets a sheet of water fall over a pane of kiln-formed glass, made especially for the project. It is uplit from the rill below, and at night the lights catch the patterns in the glass as the water falls over it.

To the side, the new wall holds cantilevered steps sunk within its structure. The steps are created out of the same granite blocks as those used on the floor. The designer says he wanted these to 'raise the question "How's that done?"', and adds: 'They look beautiful at night.' Lit with blue lights set into the wall, the steps appear as if they are floating in mid-air.

Light has been used to create this floating effect for the whole of the lower area too. This sitting area, made from granite blocks laid in regular lines, is raised up level with the

DESIGN BRIEF
- Modern courtyard
- Lighting
- Garden room

FEATURES
- Glass water-feature
- Floating patio
- Oriental-style hideaway

back door. Underneath and all around it are LED lights, which at night turn the patio into a platform floating in a sea of planting.

These floating areas are something of a trademark for Philip Nash. Sitting areas are raised up on brick piers and light spills from underneath, giving a stunning effect that works well in the smallest of areas. Even if you cannot get outside, it is worth putting the lights on just to appreciate the view. All of the lights in the garden are remote controlled, so can be operated from inside or out.

As the sitting area is raised, the planting around the edges is, at ground level, slightly sunken, which has some benefits. Soil is less apparent and, especially against the flat surface of the walls, you see the forms of the plants rather than where they come from.

An inbuilt seating area finishes off the design and reinforces the shape of the garden. The benches and table were made quite simply with outdoor marine ply and stainless steel. Underneath the seats are lines of planting.

At the top of the cantilevered steps is a jungle area with tender, evergreen plants and a path running through.

The plants are architectural and bold, with dwarf fan palms (*Chamaerops humilis*), cabbage palms (*Cordyline australis*) and grevillea (*Grevillea rosmarinifolia*). However, there are also splashes of colour at different times of the year from a variety of tulips, alliums and agapanthus. The planting up here is so dense that, looking up, you cannot see the rear of the garden and it is not clear exactly how much or, indeed, how little depth there is.

Designer's tip Inbuilt seats are a great space-saver and look very sleek. A freestanding table and chairs that could seat six would take up the entire space, but the seats here fit neatly into a corner and work with the design rather than cluttering it.

ABOVE: The walls around the sitting area, built to hold back the sloping ground, have been used to create the feeling of an outside room.

OPPOSITE, TOP LEFT: Floating granite steps are set into the new retaining sidewall.

OPPOSITE, TOP RIGHT: Purple agapanthus adds to the cool colour palette of greys and blacks.

OPPOSITE, BOTTOM LEFT: The stylish inbuilt seating area was made specially for the garden from marine ply and stainless steel.

OPPOSITE, BOTTOM RIGHT: Specially made kiln-formed glass catches the light at night as the water falls down into a rill.

Designer's tip The existing fences on the upper level were not especially pretty, so the designer used rows of a single type of climber, star jasmine (*Trachelospermum jasminoides*), to cover them. Using the same plant to cover all the walls gives unity to the design and star jasmine is a good choice for scent in this enclosed area. It is also evergreen, so cover will be year-round.

Through the planting is a path of compacted Cedec gravel, which gives an unobtrusive, natural-looking path without the loose stones of normal gravel. The path leads to a wonderful oriental-style studio at the very back of the garden. With frosted glass and modern lines, what could have been quite a prosaic building adds to the design and makes a great hideaway. At night, the studio's internal lights illuminate the glass so that the whole building glows softly.

The garden is great for older children, who can sit in it with their friends and escape to their own 'room' at the top of the garden. And, of course, it is also stylish and welcoming for adults. The difficulties of the slope at the beginning of the design process are forgotten now that

the garden is in place and, indeed, the garden would not work without it. Hiding the playroom up at the top gives an added feeling of escape and adventure. The raised plants in front of it can be seen to great effect from the house, and the enclosed courtyard, with its water feature, would not have felt so enclosed and complete without its retaining walls.

ABOVE: White agapanthus provide seasonal colour to enhance the evergreen structural planting.

RIGHT: The oriental-looking studio transforms the far end of the garden. Rather than a utilitarian structure, this design adds to the ambience.

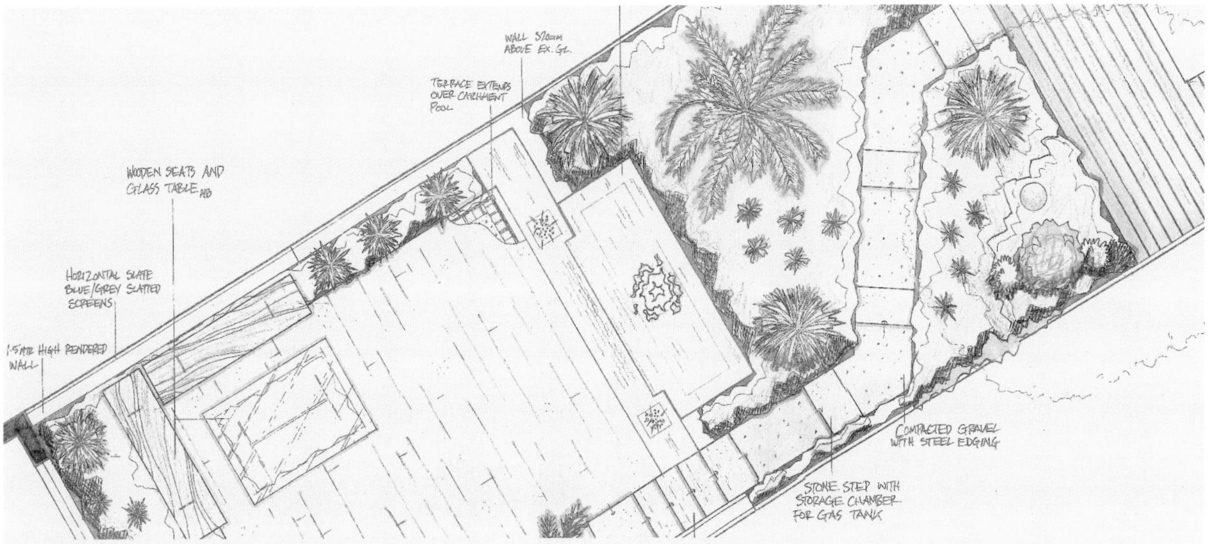
WALL 520MM ABOVE EX. GL.
TERRACE EXTENDS OVER CATCHMENT POOL
WOODEN SEATS AND GLASS TABLE
HORIZONTAL SLATE BLUE/GREY SLATTED SCREENS
1.5MTR HIGH RENDERED WALL
COMPACTED GRAVEL WITH STEEL EDGING
STONE STEP WITH STORAGE CHAMBER FOR GAS TANK

ABOVE: Philip Nash's design for the Sophisticated Rooms garden.

Employing a professional

It is often difficult to see how you can get the garden you want when you live every day with what you have. A fresh, professional eye can help here. It may be that you just need someone for a one-off consultation to get you started, or to sort out a specific problem. Or, at the other end of the scale, you may want someone to provide plans, planting schemes, to oversee the work and be involved in the ongoing development of the garden.

Choosing a designer

Personal recommendation is best, especially if you can check out an example of a particular designer's work.

Good local nurseries will know designers working in the area and should be able to point you in the direction of someone who will suit your needs.

Garden designers often exhibit or have stands at gardening shows. This is a good way of meeting several designers in one go and having an informal chat.

Most designers have websites that show pictures of their work and also reflect their style and approach.

Introductory consultation

This first meeting is for the designer to have an initial look at the garden and to discuss your needs. The designer will be accumulating information to start the design process, and you will be assessing whether the designer is right for you. Assuming you have chosen an experienced designer whose style you like, communication is the next most important thing: is the designer listening to you, and does he or she understand what you want? It sounds obvious, but if you do not click at this first meeting and feel comfortable, it may be better to find someone else. It is also important that the designer explains the process to you and, even at this early stage, talks you through all the options to achieve what you want. After the meeting, the designer will usually give you a quote for the design work discussed. Note that designers may also charge a fee for this initial meeting.

Costs

If you know how much you want to spend, it is better to tell the designer at the start. He or she can then tailor his or her design to this figure. If you are not working to a specific budget, you can wait until the quotes come in and then, if necessary, remove some items or trade down on materials.

Designer's tip Hard landscaping and manpower are usually the biggest costs in building a garden. The more hard landscaping you have, the more expensive the garden will be.

Brief

It is worth writing out a brief for the designer, either before or after the initial consultation. This could include:

- All the things you do not like about your existing garden and any plants or features that can stay or should go.
- Any problems you have noticed with the soil or any good features of the garden you would like to enhance.
- What you would like in the new garden and any preferred style.
- Sitting areas, where they should be, and how many people need to be accommodated.
- Whether you want water features, lighting or ornaments.
- How many people (including children) are in the house.
- Whether pets or children need any special provision.
- Maintenance – how keen on gardening are you?
- Other features you may want or need to include, such as vegetable areas, bins, washing lines and compost heaps.

Small.04

Height and Depth

Claire Mee
Kensington, London, 2004

This garden is typical of many small, city backyards. Below ground level, it is reached by steep steps from the ground floor of the house. Deep-set gardens like this can be very forbidding and, if you have got one that has been neglected, it is difficult to see how it could ever become a place you would want to spend time in.

This was the situation that faced designer Claire Mee when she first saw the deep well of a garden on this site. 'It was such a waste; neither the children nor the adults wanted to go outside. A central part of the brief was to encourage the four children out of the house.'

There were three main problems to overcome. First was access. The steep and rickety steps had to be changed for something more manageable and inviting. To resolve this, Claire has made each of the steps deeper and put in a handrail to make them safe for children. She has also turned them into a wonderful night-time feature. The risers are of frosted Perspex with backlights so that the entire stairway lights up.

The second problem was light. Gardens like this one, surrounded by walls and houses, can be dark. By imposing a good structure on the garden, Claire has taken an overgrown space and ordered it. 'The surrounding walls are an incredibly dominant feature of the garden. Before we started they were dark and gave a dingy feel to the area. We used a light-coloured render on the existing walls and built some new low retaining walls with the same render to divide up the space.' This lighter colour on the walls immediately lifts and lightens up the garden.

Designer's tip Rather than painting the render, Claire left it bare. A single flat coat of paint would look too overpowering in this small space, but the textured render gives a softer look that blends into the background rather than jumping forward.

The third problem was deciding what to include in this small outdoor space to encourage the children to use it. A purpose-built climbing area offered a perfect solution. It uses the depth of the area while having a small footprint on the ground so that it does not take up the whole garden. The climbing frame is built around an existing tree, which gives added interest and helps make it feel part of the garden. Because it was built for the site, the clients were able to specify exactly what they (and their children) wanted. Claire says: 'It's really not difficult to make your own climbing equipment or have it made for you, and you'll get something that fits the site and your needs perfectly. In this case, it had to work around the tree, so we had to get it made specially.' There is a hidden den area at the base and various ways to climb to a higher platform. Therefore, a climbing frame such as this one is ideal where many children (in this instance four offspring and their friends) are involved, so as to minimise bickering.

Designer's tip The climbing frame is right next to the house. You might feel that a structure like this should be positioned at the back of the garden, to hide it. However, by keeping it close to the house, when you look out you look over it, so it does not dominate the view. This works with anything you need to include in the garden, but do not want to see.

DESIGN BRIEF
• Low maintenance
• Encourage children to use the garden
• Flowers

FEATURES
• Purpose-built climbing frame
• Steps lit from behind
• Rendered wall

If you have a small garden like this, the boundaries – in this case the walls – become very important. They cannot be hidden, and probably the best way to deal with them is to look on them as an opportunity (where planting space is at a premium) to include more plants.

Obviously climbers can be used, but here a selection of trees has also been included; more than you would think would fit in a garden of this size. But trees are perfect for this space; narrow trunks take up little room on the ground and can be trained against the walls. They give an immediate maturity to the garden and height to the planting, and break up the flat areas of wall. Trees can be bought in just about any size, and you can specify how tall a trunk you want before the branches start, though it is worth taking advice about which will respond well to your situation.

Because the climbing frame is contained in one corner of the garden, the rest of the space can be more adult-orientated. Claire has created a cosy sitting area surrounded by raised beds. The built-in benches help to define the structure and give seating without clutter, and the raised beds, with their rendered walls, form the structure of this garden and divide up the space. They provide the perfect space for soft-flowing plants such as the daisy-like Mexican fleabane (*Erigeron karvinskianus*), fuchsia (*Fuchsia* 'Annabelle Stubbs') and a variety of early flowering aquilegias.

Designer's tip Raised beds will help if you have dominating walls. They break up the flat planes of the walls so that, instead of starting from ground level, the visible walls start from 50 centimetres (20 inches) or so off the ground.

This garden, while small, has a lot of potential in its height. The boundary walls provide extra growing room and also create proportions that allow tall structures and plants. Claire has made the most of this dimension in her design. The climbing frame is tall and thin: were the garden not surrounded by walls, it would look out of place. But nestled against the house it blends into the dimensions of the area.

Similarly, Claire has taken the opportunity to use taller trees that can grow upwards, use the height and soften the boundaries. If the boundaries were not there, the trees would also look out of place. Within the harsh confines of the area, the designer has brought in a soft yet structured garden that meets the needs of both children and adults.

ABOVE: The walls have been softened with render, which gives an earthy, textured look.

ABOVE The garden is approached by steep steps, but down below the new low wall helps to create a better-proportioned space for the sitting area beyond.

ABOVE: Cordoned fruit and abundant, flowery planting add another layer of softness to this walled city-garden.

Vertical planting

Rather than seeing walls as a problem, look on them as an opportunity for extra planting space. Climbers are the first choice for this. Most climbers will need support – either wires or a trellis – to grow upwards. And in many ways this is a good thing, as you can decide where they will grow, and they will not impinge on the wall itself. If you go for self-clingers like ivy or climbing hydrangea (*Hydrangea anomala subsp. petiolaris*)**,** support is not necessary. However, climbers like these have a tendency to run away and will damage loose render or pointing.

The following are good climbers for a small space:

Armand clematis (*Clematis armandii*)
An evergreen with large leaves and vanilla-scented flowers in spring.

Kolomikta (*Actinidia kolomikta*)
A deciduous climber with cream- and pink-tipped leaves.

Chocolate vine (*Akebia quinata*)
A semi-evergreen with pretty leaves and purple, chocolate-scented flowers in spring.

Honeysuckle (*Lonicera periclymenum* 'Graham Thomas')
Scented summer flowers that open white and turn yellow.

Clematis 'Purpurea Plena Elegans'
Late-flowering clematis with beautiful red/purple double flowers.

Trees can also be used against walls, and espaliered (fan-trained) fruit trees are ideal for this. In this garden, two pears (*Pyrus communis* 'Beurré Hardy' and *Pyrus communis* 'Doyenné du Comice') and one apple tree (*Malus* 'Canada Grey Queen')

have been used. These will provide blossom in spring and fruit in the autumn. One caveat – fruit trees need pollinating in order to set fruit. It is a complicated business to get the right trees together, so it is worth buying from a good nursery and taking their advice on which ones you need.

Small.05

Mediterranean Modern
Tommaso del Buono and Paul Gazerwitz
Islington, London, 2003

The following seems really obvious when you say it, but in a way so much so that you tend to forget it: hard landscaping is great at providing permanent structure and definition, and soft landscaping – planting – is great at giving colour, change and life to a garden. And although plants can form strong lines, the most powerful statements come from bricks and stone, concrete and render.

At one end of the spectrum are unrelenting lines and, at the other, planting that is diaphanous and abundant, changes with the seasons and provides dancing informality. In this garden, these two extremes butt together to great effect. The design team, Tommaso del Buono and Paul Gazerwitz, have exploited the differences in shape, form and texture to create a stunning garden, and proved that the most effective contrasts come from extremes.

The garden is small, but in many ways this works in favour of the contrast. On a larger plot it would be more nebulous, less intense. Here, surrounded by walls and buildings, the garden's stonework can be used surgically to cut across and surround the area. In a larger space this would not work as well, and there would be other things to distract from the scene. But as it is, the concentrated juxtaposition is controlled and works in perfect balance.

The garden was formed when a striking new house was built on a small city-plot. Floor-to-ceiling glass enclosed in a concrete case, the house is beautiful in its simplicity. And with so much glass, the views out to the garden here were a major consideration. The owners wanted to see the seasons changing, and were inspired by Mediterranean courtyards. But they also wanted a garden that fitted with the Modernist style of the house.

The solution was to enclose the garden with the architectural, formal and modern, and centrally, where perhaps a lawn might have been, to create vast beds of flowers.

To give a seamless join between house and garden, the same limestone has been used on the floor outside as inside. When the huge glass doors are thrown back, there really is no distinction between house and garden. Limestone is a wonderful material to use here. It is reflective, light and modern, gives an air of the Mediterranean to the area, and also provides a foil for the brightly coloured plants spilling over from the beds.

The abundance of planting in two large beds just outside the kitchen creates the first impression of the garden as you walk out to it. There are euphorbias (*Euphorbia characias* subsp. *characias* 'Humpty Dumpty'), irises (*Iris* 'Florentina'), lavenders (*Lavandula angustifolia* 'Royal Purple') and geraniums (*Geranium pratense* 'Mrs Kendall Clark'). The beds are large for the area, but in proportion, and defiantly held in place by the limestone. There is room for a great variety of planting that can provide interest all year round. Bergenias, grasses and sedums will all be good throughout the winter; in spring the show starts with a variety of irises, sisyrinchiums and euphorbias, and is carried on through summer with lavenders, nepeta, verbena and peonies.

Designer's tip Running limestone stepping-stones through beds not only allows access to tend to the plants, but also, in the winter, when the planting is sparser, gives pattern and structure to an area.

DESIGN BRIEF
• Link with newly built house
• Planting that changes through the seasons
• A family-friendly garden
• Outdoor eating area

FEATURES
• Water feature
• Inbuilt bench
• Pleached pears (*Pyrus calleryana* 'Chanticleer')

Designer's tip If space is very tight, it is tempting to put outdoor tables right outside the kitchen. Avoid this if possible, as two tables, effectively next to each other on either side of the glass, will look strange.

Over to the side, an inbuilt limestone bench maintains the formality and provides a horizontal accent to the garden. The bench is also the basis for a water feature of stunning simplicity. At the rear of the bench's far end is a slit through which a sheet of water flows out, across the seat, before falling to a pool below. The clients wanted to be able to hear the sound of water in the garden, and this heavy curtain of water makes a wonderful noise as it falls. The long pool carries on back towards the house, its surface broken by three perfectly proportioned limestone blocks. The bench and water feature enclose and surround the sitting area, which houses a large table and chairs.

At the back of the garden, alongside a studio where the owners can work away from the house, is an enormous ash tree that provides a shady corner for a bench. Shade-loving box (*Buxus sempervirens*) has been used to form a cloud hedge at the front of the area and behind this enormous acanthus flowers tower above.

As with most small, city spaces, the surrounding walls are a major influence on the garden and there is always a risk that they will dominate the space. This garden has the benefit of having quite beautiful walls, so it was not necessary to hide them. The glass of the house and the rich-coloured wood of the studio form the front and back walls. To one side is a brick wall, and to the other a gorgeous concrete one. 'Concrete' and 'gorgeous' are not often used in the same sentence, but this wall has a delicate texture and colour and works so beautifully with the stark white limestone.

Although the walls did not need to be hidden, they did require some softening, so formal planting was used to break up their lines. Three evergreen strawberry trees (*Arbutus unedo*) have been placed in pots along one wall, and facing these is a line of pleached pears (*Pyrus calleryana* 'Chanticleer') that carries on around the house. The pears have nearly 2 metres (6.5 feet) of clear stems before branching, which give a strong repeated upright pattern along the wall. Above, the foliage forms a clean line of screening.

Designer's tip Pleached trees are wonderful for providing instant height. They are effectively hedges on stilts, and are great for screening without taking up room on the ground. Pears like those here will also give white blossom in the spring. A warning, though, they do need to be kept trimmed and this work, at height, is not always easy.

Good design seems so obvious and so simple. But finding that obvious solution in the first place is one of the arts of garden design. Another is taking the design idea and making it work on the ground. The proportions, the materials, the use of space all have to be right to create a garden that, like this one, looks like it was meant to be.

ABOVE LEFT: The wooden exterior of the studio contrasts with the concrete sidewall.

ABOVE RIGHT: The seating area has been placed slightly away from the kitchen so the table here and the kitchen table do not sit side by side.

OPPOSITE: A 'cloud' clipped box hedge (*Buxus sempervirens*) sits along the top of the retaining wall, softening the hard lines and increasing the feeling of seclusion.

ABOVE: Light-coloured limestone paving contrasts beautifully with the abundant planting.

RIGHT: Pleached pears (*Pyrus calleryana* 'Chanticleer') have been used as a screen above the height of the existing wall, and provide lovely repeated verticals with their stems.

BELOW: The sheer exuberance of the planting in the tidy courtyard has an uplifting and ever-changing presence.

Small trees

If you have a small garden, do not assume trees will be too big for it. Small trees give height and screening and take up little room at ground level. However, there are some to avoid. Huge ones, obviously, and some are too garish. In addition, purple-leaved trees can be overbearing through the summer and cast too dense shade. If you are worried about root run near the house, plant the tree in a container. This will also limit its size.

Lines of trees can look stunning, whether in containers, as here, or in the ground. My favourite is amelanchier – it looks good for most of the year with spring blossom and autumn colour. A multistemmed tree will also provide excellent architecture in winter.

Following is a list of trees that can work well in small gardens:

Winter-flowering cherry (*Prunus* x *subhirtella* 'Autumnalis Rosea') This will provide pink flowers in mild spells through the winter.

Snowy mespilus (*Amelanchier lamarckii*) This has white spring blossom and autumn colour.

Strawberry tree (*Arbutus unedo*) An evergreen with white autumn flowers and red, strawberry-like berries.

Japanese maple (*Acer palmatum* 'Sango-kaku') Another star, it has lovely pink-yellow autumn colour and coral-pink shoots during winter.

Judas tree (*Cercis siliquastrum*) This has late-spring pink blossom and heart-shaped leaves.

Chinese dogwood (*Cornus kousa* var. *chinensis*) Large white 'flowers' (it is the bracts, not the flowers, that you see) appear in early summer, followed by beautiful red-purple autumn leaves.

RIGHT: Multistemmed snowy mespilus (*Amelanchier lamarckii*).

Medium

M Introduction

Medium-sized back gardens are what most of us have. Sometimes it feels like the worst of all worlds. They are not big enough to be really exciting, but they are big enough to make you feel guilty if you do not do anything with them, do not mow the lawn or see to the flowers.

However, as the gardens in this section show, it is possible to do exceptional things with the average. Two of the gardens here make strong use of rendered walls, and these are wonderful for dividing up areas and creating different 'rooms' and a sense of discovery.

There is also room for larger playthings to be included that do not then dominate the garden. In the Offbeat garden, a large trampoline has been sunk into the far corner in a way that does not overpower the garden. A frame has been included in the Water, Light and Walls garden, on to which can be put a hammock for adults or a swing for children.

With more space and different elements, pathways through the garden become important. This is something to think about if you are designing your own garden – how will you move around the area, do you need hard paths or will it be possible to walk over the grass in all weathers? A good idea for family gardens is rolled gravel. It is not loose in the way normal gravel is, so children will not be able to throw it about or put it in their mouths, and it fits well in modern areas and reflects light beautifully.

BELOW: Rendered walls are a wonderful, modern way to divide up areas and create interest.

At this size of garden, mainten-ance starts to be an issue. If you are going to be looking after the garden yourself, it can make a huge difference if you can design it to keep maintenance down.

In general the rule is that the more planting you have, the more maintenance there will be. Hard landscaping is more expensive to install, but easier to look after, and will impose order on to the garden, however bad you are at gardening.

Lawns count as planting and do require work. Two of the gardens in this section do not have lawns, and work very well without them. If you do include a lawn, make the shape as simple as possible so that there are no intricate curves to mow around. A mowing strip (a line of hard landscaping set slightly below the level of the lawn) around the edge will mean you do not have to edge it for it to look neat.

Before any planting, get rid of the perennial weeds. If you do not mind using chemicals, spray them off (a few treatments will probably be necessary to get rid of all traces of them). Improving the quality of the soil will also help new plants get established and grow well to drown out weeds.

Where you do have plants, the more evergreen and structural types you have the lower the maintenance will be. This used to be called shrub planting, but this term has now gone out of fashion. However, shrubs, bamboos and trees all look after themselves to a large degree.

ABOVE: Block planting gives a strong look, and is easier to maintain than more traditional, cottage-garden-style planting.

Planting in blocks will be easier to look after than a cottage-like effect with plants dotted around. In the Water, Light and Walls garden, the palette of plants has been kept small and each type has been planted in large drifts. Planting this way means you can tackle each drift in one hit and, with only a few different types of plants to tend, not too many hits will be needed.

Put in plants that require the same level and type of maintenance. One of the lowest-maintenance planting schemes is perennials, which will hold their form through winter and need cutting down to the ground in the early spring (see the plant guide at the back of the book for examples). This means that, apart from a little titivation, the garden work can be done in one hit, once a year.

Some people swear by putting a membrane down on planted beds and covering it with bark chippings to keep weeds at bay. But unless this is done well, the membrane has a habit of rearing up and looking ugly. Another way to reduce weeds is to really fill the beds with planting so that your plants crowd out the weeds and keep them down.

Automatic irrigation systems can help. This is especially important if you may be away for a while during the summer. Thin hosepipes are snaked around the ground below the plants in many of the gardens in this section to take the pain out of watering.

It is easy to make a mess in the garden. Pruning and pulling up weeds is not so bad, it is the tidying up afterwards that is a drag. Small dumping grounds around the garden can help here, so that you do not have to go all the way to a compost bin or take out the rubbish every time you pull up a weed.

Containers are high maintenance and, technically, if you want a low-maintenance garden, they should be banned. This said, many people do not mind looking after containers, even if they do not like gardening, as they seem a manageable and pleasant way to potter.

Medium.01

Water, Light and Walls
Paul Dracott
Barnes, London, 2004

If there is one garden that sums up what this book is all about, it is this one. Out went the lawn, out went the climbing frame, out went the dull little borders. In their place are structural walls, exciting planting, water and light. And, perhaps surprisingly, the children play in this garden much, much more than they did in the old traditional one.

Paul Dracott has created a garden that works for both adults and children: 'Before we started, the garden was a typical 1950s area with a garage at the back and a central lawn. There was a play frame, but the children rarely used it. Now they are always out there.'

The design of the garden had two main thrusts. One was to fit with the new extension on the house; the other to provide a tactile outdoor environment for the children while not compromising on style.

The new extension with double-height glass brought a modern twist to a 1930s house and opened it up to the garden. To link house and garden, Paul has used the same decking on the floor of the patio as that used inside, the decking boards running the same way so that the lines carry on through the glass and into the garden. He has also carefully observed the interior and reflected its modern, clean look in the garden.

Paul has also linked garden and house in a more fundamental way.

The overall layout of the garden has been designed on a grid, taking its proportions from the house. Here, the central measurement was taken from rear doors, which are 1.2 metres (4 feet) wide. All the dimensions of the garden are this size or multiples of it. As Paul says: 'This relates the garden to the house and creates a garden with restful, ordered proportions.'

Paul always looks very carefully at a house, its design, proportions and how it has been decorated: 'The house drives the design for the garden so that the two work together, flow easily and the garden doesn't look just stuck on.'

Designer's tip Using the proportions of the house within the garden is a good way to achieve a garden that works with its surrounds. This idea came from John Brookes, one of the greatest modern British garden designers, who has written about it in many books. It is a fairly simple and pretty foolproof way to get a ground-plan design that works with the scale of the house, so that, as John says, 'proportionally they tie together to create a room outside'.

Proportions are particularly important in a garden like this, where the space has been divided up so strongly with walls. The division was necessary once the decision was made not to have any grass. 'It's quite a big space to have without a lawn, so we divided up the space with a rendered wall running in three sections across the garden.'

The walls not only divide up the space; they are the beginning of the story of the tactile garden. The main dividing wall creates two distinct areas in the garden where children can play, hide and discover.

This main wall also holds the water feature. A lip of water falls from the wall into a pond below, which, covered with a metal grille, forms the walkway through the garden and gives access to the second area. 'The children love to sit and watch the fish below them and, of course, it's safe for them,' says Paul.

DESIGN BRIEFS
- A garden for the family
- A sensory garden
- To complement house

FEATURES
- Fish pond
- No lawn
- Perspex panels in walls

Providing stimulation for the children was a major part of the brief for this garden. 'We wanted a tactile space with things to stimulate all the senses, and the falling water and fish provide both sounds and sights for the children.'

To the rear of the garden are things specifically designed for the children, but which do not seem out of place here. There is a frame for swings and, in an area with tactile vinyl on the floor, a sandpit.

Designer's tip The swing frame here is a great space-saving idea, as either a swing for children or a hammock for adults can be hooked on to it.

The planting is another element of the design that works for the children and the adults. The plants are exciting and colourful, and as a result the children bring their toy animals outdoors and pretend they are in the jungle. Gunneras (*Gunnera manicata*) have been put in with the express purpose of having their leaves broken off to be used in play. This planting, of bold colours in bold drifts, also works with the modern design and is relatively low maintenance. Black-eyed Susan (*Rudbeckia fulgida* var. *sullivantii* 'Goldsturm') and grasses like miscanthus (*Miscanthus sinensis*) and pennisetum (*Pennisetum villosum*) are used in large blocks.

Because there are only a few different types of plant it is quite easy to keep on top of things and it is really just a case of cutting down all the plants to the ground in late winter and waiting for them to re-emerge again in spring.

'There are also,' Paul points out, 'very few weeds. These plants form a dense mat so they keep out weeds, certainly from June onwards.'

The planting at the rear of the garden is greener and less colourful than on the terrace. Paul points out: 'The terrace is hot and south facing, and I wanted this to be a more stimulating area. At the rear there are fewer flowers and the whole feel is more restful.'

All of this would be enough to make a wonderful garden, but there is an extra dimension – lighting. Paul is well known for his inventive use of lighting. Here, he has used lots of coloured lights in the garden for the children (and I suspect the adults enjoy them too). Lights are used to cast shadows on the walls, and red and blue lights are used in the pond. My favourites are the lights that shine against the Perspex panels. When the lights shine through the plants on to these panels, they project shapes that are visible from the other side, and have been designed so that the children can use the effects to make their own shadow play.

So the lighting looks wonderful, and has been turned into a game for the children. This sums up the fusion of needs that have been responded to in order to create a true family garden here. It shows that children do not have to be shunted off to a corner of the garden, and that the garden does not have to be compromised by their needs. In garden design, as in other areas of design, both children and adults respond to exciting composition and stimulating spaces.

ABOVE: Clean, light walls clearly define the structure of the garden and contrast with the soft planting.

LEFT: Busy and bright planting is used on the warm, south-facing terrace.

OPPOSITE: The walls divide the garden space into well-proportioned rooms based on the external dimensions of the house.

OVERLEAF: The water feature takes on an even more exciting dimension after dark, with coloured uplighters shining through the water.

Lighting

Lighting is an exciting and upcoming area of garden design. People are now asking for lighting more often; 10 years ago no one did. This is partly because people these days like to eat outside, but also because of the more recent fashion in interior design of having no window dressing, which allows a better view of the garden from the house. People are also realising that lighting can create a wonderful view, especially in the winter.

Designer Paul Dracott offers the following lighting tips:

- Think about what will be in the garden in winter, and what can be used for lighting effects.
- Light the background plants in white for structure, and then highlight with coloured lights.
- Do not use too many different colours – three at most.
- Blue works really well to highlight steelwork or water.
- From the main viewpoint of the garden, you should not see the light source. It is the effects of the lights you want to see, not the bright source.
- Light the foreground and the background, but keep the midground dark; if there is too much lighting the picture begins to look one-dimensional.
- Even if you are not putting lighting in when you do your garden, put the cables down so that there is provision there to add it later.
- You can use light in different ways. Uplighting – positioning lights under trees and structures – is particularly effective in the winter. Shadowing can be created by shining light through strong forms and projecting on to flat surfaces, and grazing by shining light along the surface of a wall to bring out its texture. For a moonlight effect, you will need to shine lights on to the ground. And you can light up steps using, for example, strip lights or fibre-optics.

Medium.02

Meadow on a Roof
Paula Ryan
Canning Town, London, 2003

For a roof garden, this is a very large area. 'It's about the size of a normal city garden,' says its designer Paula Ryan. 'But it was just a big blank terrace.'

The challenge was to fill the space without overcrowding it, to give meaning to different areas, and to turn it into a garden that could be enjoyed. For this, Paula has put in enormous planters, 1 metre (3.2 feet) wide and up to 7 metres (23 feet) long. These divide up the space and provide seas of colour and height on the flat roof-space.

Two distinct areas have been formed: the dining space for adults and the playing space for children. They are marked quite subtly, but the feeling of each is different. Part of the adults' space is covered by a pergola that provides a feeling of enclosure. There is also a change in floor materials. The existing pavers have been left in place for the dining area, but a raised-deck platform has been formed around the water feature to give this 'playing' space a different feel. The raised decking does not extend right to the edge; Paula has been careful to leave a level circuit around the whole area where the children can use their bicycles.

Around the corner and closed off for safety is a storage area for tools, which also houses children's playthings.

Another ingenious safety aspect is that the raised beds have been kept a metre (3.2 feet) away from the roof edges, so that even if the children climb on to the beds, they cannot use them as a launch pad to get over the sides. This gap also means that children can hide and play all around the beds, and adults can get right to the edges to look out at the stunning views.

Designer's tip Plastic sandpits might not seem ideal if you are trying to create a beautiful garden, but they have a lot going for them. The main benefit is that they are movable, so if you do not want to see them they can be stored away, and when children grow out of them they are easy to remove completely. Also, sandpits almost inevitably get very wet, whether from play or being left open, and plastic ones can be tipped out easily. Because they tend to be small, a single bag of sand will refill them.

The beds are made of marine ply with a softwood frame, sealed inside with bitumen and painted. Paula admits that these will not last for ever, 'but it's the nature of this sort of garden where weight is an issue'. Structural issues loom large with roof gardens, and keeping the weight down is an enormous constraint. This development was newly built, which meant it was relatively easy to talk to the engineer who designed the building about safety and loads. The largest and, therefore, heaviest bed is placed above the steel supports of the flat below.

Another issue with roof gardens is access – how to bring in heavy and large materials? This can be done in three ways: in the lift, by stairs, or hoisting them up the side of the building. On a lower building, the last would be possible, but here the height of the roof terrace meant this was not feasible. The only access was therefore through a small passenger lift or up the stairs – and nothing over a couple of metres long would fit in the lift. 'We managed to design it so that only the long wood for the pergola had to

DESIGN BRIEF
• Child safe
• Minimalist and simple
• Contrast with urban skyline
• Tight budget

FEATURES
• Large planters
• Water feature
• Pergola

be carried up the stairs – the rest was brought up in short lengths and assembled up on top,' says Paula.

For obvious reasons, this is a very outward-looking garden. The views from all sides are wonderful. With this in mind, Paula designed the low, curving, copper water feature to blend in with the skyline without impinging upon it. It gives interest and reflects the light, and is a big hit with the children. 'We couldn't put pebbles or slate chips at the base as the children might throw them,' Paula says, 'so we used slate slabs to cover the reservoir.' It is raised up within a planter so all the mechanics are above ground level, but hidden away.

The real star of the garden, though, is the planting. It is soft and abundant, designed to look meadow-like and wild. Summer is when this garden is used the most, and the planting reflects this with waves of colour throughout the season. Bright dots of deep-red Macedonian scabious (*Knautia macedonica*) dance through golden grasses like calamagrostis (*Calamagrostis* x *acutiflora* 'Stricta'). The tones are earthy and gold, with yellow fern-leaf yarrow (*Achillea filipendulina* 'Cloth of Gold') and rich red day lilies (*Hemerocallis* 'Stafford'). Where screening is needed,

bamboos (*Phyllostachys aureosulcata* f. *aureocaulis*) and tall miscanthus grasses (*Miscanthus sinensis*) have been planted en masse.

What is immediately striking on entering this garden is how huge the sky is. And, from this vantage point, towering above the surrounding buildings and looking out over the city skyline, the full panorama unfolds beneath you. The garden does nothing to intrude upon this view, and it would be silly to lose this grand sweep by introducing tall features. And though this leaves the garden open to the elements, it is a pay-off. Rather than using architectural plants and competing with the view, the planting here provides a huge contrast with the urban surroundings. All around is industry and architecture, but within the garden the planting forms a meadow-like oasis in the sky.

OPPOSITE: The garden has many attractions for children. The water feature is a big draw and, with no standing water, safe for the little ones. In addition, a clear space has been left around the containers, mainly for safety, but it also makes a great bicycle track.

BELOW: The 'adult' area is subtly marked by a change in floor materials and the pergola overhead.

ABOVE: The planters soften the garden and bring a meadow-like feel without interfering with the wonderful views.

LEFT: The low, curving, copper water feature is robust enough to cope with small children.

BELOW: When not being used by the children, the area is sophisticated and calm.

ABOVE: Purple coneflower (*Echinacea purpurea*).

Late-summer plants

If you are planting for summer, do not get carried away with June- or even July-flowering plants. Often the warmest days are in August and September, and it is just depressing if everything is past its best and the only thing to look forward to is decline.

If you have to make a choice, go for late summer- and autumn-flowering plants over earlier ones. Spring and early summer are so full of life anyway that a garden can hardly fail to look good. But later in the year it is important to have something with potential and which looks fresh. The plants below could be planted together in a border, and the flower colours are mainly in the pinks and purples so will blend well.

Strawberry tree (*Arbutus unedo*)
This evergreen strawberry tree produces white flowers in autumn, just as the previous year's fruits are turning red.

Californian lilac (*Ceanothus* 'Autumnal Blue')
This Californian lilac is an evergreen shrub with blue flowers in the autumn.

***Caryopteris x clandonensis* 'First Choice'**
A very elegant shrub with deep-blue flowers in late summer.

Chinese plumbago (*Ceratostigma willmottianum*)
This small shrub has blue flowers in late summer.

Japanese anemone 'Hadspen Abundance' (*Anemone hupehensis* 'Hadspen Abundance')
A tall, late summer-flowering perennial with dark-pink flowers.

Purple coneflower (*Echinacea purpurea*)
This has large, purple, daisy-like flowers in late summer and autumn. Even after the flowers have gone, the seed heads look good.

Aster 'Mönch (*Aster* x *frikartii* 'Mönch')
This has purple, daisy-like flowers with yellow centres.

Liriope muscari
This is an evergreen, grass-like plant that has purple flowers in the autumn.

Bowden Cornish lily (*Nerine bowdenii*)
An autumn-flowering bulb with a delicate pink flower. It is dormant in the summer, but will pop up in autumn to produce flowers. It is a little tender, so needs to be in a sheltered position.

Ivy-leaved cyclamen (*Cyclamen hederifolium*)
Another bulb, this one is a low-growing plant that in autumn can carpet areas with pink flowers.

Medium.03

Offbeat
James Fraser
Surrey, 2003

'Why does everything have to be straight? In nature, everything flows; straight lines create tension.' This was the response from James Fraser, of Avant Gardener, when I asked him why everything in his gardens is wonky. Clean, straight lines and uncluttered layouts hold no appeal – 'There's nothing minimalist about nature'. This is a man who has definite ideas about gardens.

His ideas are based on using what is around us to inspire gardens, being ecologically aware, categorically not using straight lines, and enjoying the space. 'Gardens are fun – you can't take them too seriously.' James's gardens are full of plants; the lines are informal and idiosyncratic and they are indeed a great deal of fun.

So, rather than draw up plans with rulers, compasses and set squares – implements that lead most designers to formality of some sort – James gets in the materials and fashions his design on site: 'We do a specification for the materials, so we can get a budget approved, but once we get out there we go with the flow.' This ensures his gardens have a handmade, handcrafted quality that is quite unique.

The feeling is enhanced by James's use of reclaimed materials. He scours demolition sites to find suitable pieces of wood. Their worn, irregular feel fits perfectly with his style and helps to create this reconstructed look.

James wants to get as much out of the site as possible – for people and for plants. In this garden, the lawn was part of the client's brief. However, if James had been given completely free rein he may well have used the entire space for planting. But, as the garden needed to accommodate three children, a lawn seemed like a good idea.

The sunken trampoline in the corner is also specifically for the children who, even now, in their teens, like to use it – if only for lying on. When the children move on, the hole under the trampoline is destined to become a pond.

Designer's tip Sinking a trampoline is a great way to hide it and to make it slightly safer for children to use. This is fairly simple to do, but requires a lot of digging, and the sides should be shored up with wooden battens. If there is room, it is a great idea to mound the earth up around the sides to create surrounding grassy banks.

Around the edges of the garden, the planting has been retained in raised beds made from large, different-sized pieces of reclaimed wood. The beds were carefully built by James to provide the ideal growing environment for plants. Raised beds mean controlling the compost, feed and water the plants get is easier than at ground level. The plants here are as unusual as the construction. James has used subtropical ones like purple houmspara (*Pseudopanax* 'Purpureus'), hoheria (*Hoheria angustifolia*), acacia (*Acacia privissima*) and myrtle (*Myrtus apiculata*) to form the backbone of his palette. 'We don't use English natives. Most of the gardens we do are small gardens in London and they all have restraints with space. These plants will give winter interest; they're evergreen but they're not butch.' Summer interest comes from plants like the large golden-leaved Indian bean trees (*Catalpa bignonioides* 'Aurea'), the banana plant (*Musa basjoo*) and perennials like honey bush (*Melianthus major*) and verbena (*Verbena bonariensis*).

The edges of the raised beds provide seating around the garden for children and adults. They are interspersed with

DESIGN BRIEF
• Terrace
• Sitting area at rear
• Lawn

FEATURES
• Sunken trampoline
• Raised beds
• Pergola

walkways, platforms and hidden seating areas all made from reclaimed hardwoods and built in the same irregular way.

Reclaimed wood has also been used for the pergola down one side of the garden. A pergola sounds quite traditional, but here it has been given the Fraser twist: one side is taller than the other, and it zigzags down the garden. Under the pergola, Italian porphyry cobbles are laid randomly to form a path. They jiggle about in a haphazard way, but although unplanned the layout is not unconsidered. At the end of the pergola is a semi-hidden seating area with a large table and chairs. These are quite normal, 'not built by us,' says James.

The three compost bins were built by Avant Gardener and are, of course, wonky. Set at angles to each other, they fit in with the lines of the garden. James considers these the most important item in the garden, as the compost from them feeds the plants.

Designer's tip It is tempting to put compost bins in a far-flung area of the garden, but they are much more likely to be used if they are near where the rubbish is made. If you do not have space to hide compost bins in the central part of the garden, try having small hidden heaps around the garden that can be moved every few weeks to the bins.

To create a garden like this requires a great deal of confidence in your designer. And getting it right requires a great deal of skill. The garden is created in situ, and there is little room for manoeuvre if it is not right. When I asked one of the clients here what brief she had given the designer, she smiled and said: 'You don't give James a brief.' James has built gardens for these clients before, and they have built up a level of trust and understanding that allows him freedom to experiment. James understands their tastes and needs, and they trust him to deliver.

BELOW LEFT: Golden-leaved Indian bean trees (*Catalpa bignonioides* 'Aurea') give an exotic, large-leaved look.

BELOW RIGHT: The wonky pergola will eventually be covered in climbers.

OPPOSITE: The handcrafted appearance of the terrace steps was achieved using reclaimed wood.

ABOVE: The sunken trampoline still holds appeal even though the children are now teenagers.

LEFT: The compost bins, like the rest of the garden, follow their own lines.

ABOVE: Lawns have their uses even in less traditional gardens.

Lawns

It was decided early on that the lawn would have to stay in this garden. And you can see why. Grass provides an ideal play surface, and sometimes children just need space to run about and play games. But it does present a design problem. You immediately have a large, flat surface that needs to be placed quite centrally in the garden to allow room for plants around the edges.

If you are going to have a lawn, one of the first decisions is whether to have a formal or informal shape and feel to it.

Formal lawns tend to be harder work. It is more important that they look perfect, and so the edges will need trimming with more assiduity. Less formal lawns can drift into wildflower areas, and a little imperfection here or there will not spoil the look too much. Below are some steps towards a perfect lawn. There is more you can do, but these should be enough to give a good return.

The more often you cut the grass, the better it will be. In the great formal public gardens, grass is cut three or four times a week. You do not have to go to this extreme, but you should try to avoid leaving it too long; if you cut down more than a third of the height of the grass in one go, it will weaken the grass and cause browning.

Having said that, leave the lawn in spells of very dry hot weather when cutting might stress the grass.

Feed the lawn in spring and autumn. Use a slow-release fertiliser, which is high in nitrogen, in spring, and an autumn feed that is high in phosphate and potash.

Weed-kill if necessary, and if you do not mind using chemicals. The chemicals will work best when the weeds are growing strongly and it is not too dry, so spring is usually best. Be careful not to use chemicals in windy weather, or nearby plants may suffer. If you do not want to use chemicals, weeds can be controlled by regular cutting, raking and removal by hand.

Clearing off fallen leaves and scarifying (raking vigorously) in autumn will help to keep the lawn looking good.

Medium.04

Stainless Steel and Stone

Richard York and David Davies
Northamptonshire, 2003

The work on the patio of this garden formed the first stage of an ongoing project to develop the whole garden. Sitting areas like this are often a good place to start if you want to do your garden over time. You will get a lot of use out of them, and feel that you have made some progress. However, on the other hand, seating areas are often the most expensive part of a garden design.

The paved area here is sunk below the surrounding walkways and uses the changes in level to good effect. The drop in levels has been exploited by using a rill that falls down the steps at the end of the patio area in a stainless-steel trough that is bent to the shape of the steps. Behind the uprights are blue lights, set above the water line, so that they are easier to maintain and replace. The rill is 10 metres (33 feet) long and falls across the patio and into an organic pond that breaks up what would otherwise have been a large expanse of paving.

Designer's tip A long rill like this will need a large pump, and an underground reservoir that can hold all the water in the system so that when it is switched off it does not overflow.

At the end of the rill, where it reaches the pond, large stones have been used to make sure there is no standing water. Also for safety, railings were needed all around the sunken area, and these have been done beautifully with stainless steel along the top to pick up on the stainless steel in the rill. The railings were designed by the client and give,

as one of the designers, Richard York, points out, 'a really enclosed feeling from down below, though when you go up to the next level you don't really notice them'.

Another feature of the garden is the way old and new have been combined. The walls around the sunken area are traditional stone, but this has been juxtaposed with large black sandstone paving and the modern lines of the rill.

Designer's tip It is not just the material you use on the floor that will give a particular effect. How you lay the stones will also affect the overall look. Larger paving stones will give a more unified feel to the area. The more regular the pattern, the more modern it will appear. Alternatively, randomly laid stones create a cottage-like feel. In the garden here, the paving is laid in lines, which gives a more modern appearance.

Up on the terrace, above the patio, is another beautiful combination of old and new in the gabions holding up a pergola. These are steel-mesh uprights filled with stone. 'We thought about brick pillars or green oak, but the gabions seemed to work the best. Stone is a well-used local material for houses and it seemed right to reflect this,' say the designers. The gabions are, unusually, made of stainless steel, not the usual galvanised steel. This meant that they were more expensive, but they look more modern and are more in keeping with the garden. In addition, rather than just filling them with rubble, the insides are carefully constructed with Cotswold stone, laid in like a dry-stone wall with each piece carefully placed.

The use of colour in this garden is immediately striking. The owners do not have a lot of time for gardening, so the planting could not be too high maintenance. Block planting of bold colours has been used, and there is a rolling colour

DESIGN BRIEF
- Area for entertaining
- Colour
- Safe for children

FEATURES
- Rill coming down steps
- Gabions
- Stainless-steel water feature

scheme throughout the year. Cottage-garden plants are in bold blocks. Daphne (*Daphne mezereum*), planted en masse, starts off the colour in the early part of the year. In late summer the colours are bold and bright with black-eyed Susan (*Rudbeckia fulgida* var. *sullivantii* 'Goldsturm'), penstemon (*Penstemon* 'Sour Grapes') and crocosmia (*Crocosmia* 'Lucifer').

Designer's tip Planting in blocks reduces maintenance. Rudbeckias, for example, can just be snipped down in late winter with a pair of shears and, if you can do this over large areas of planting at the same time, it takes a lot of the grunt work out of gardening.

RIGHT: A channel of water falls down the steps and across the patio to a small pond.

BELOW: Bold swathes of planting give colour throughout the summer.

OPPOSITE: Stainless-steel gabions have been carefully filled with Cotswold stone.

OVERLEAF: A lavender hedge softens the stainless-steel railing.

ABOVE: Globe thistle (*Echinops ritro* 'Veitch's Blue') and montbretia (*Crocosmia* 'Lucifer')

Colour in the garden

There are no strict rules regarding how to use colour in your garden, any more than there are rules about the colours you should wear or the ones you should use to paint the inside of your house – it is a matter of personal taste. However, just like the paint on the wall of your house, colour does have an enormous impact on a garden, the way it feels and its dynamic.

Playing with colours is wonderful fun. One thing I used to do in quiet moments when I worked in a garden centre was to pick up containers of plants and try out different combinations. Unexpected glories came from this simple exercise – colours have different hues and tones, and it is surprising what will work together.

By wandering around a garden centre trying out different colour combinations of flowers, rather than foliage, you can be pretty certain they will be in flower at the same time when they are in your garden.

Though there are no hard and fast rules as to right and wrong, the colour wheel is a useful guide if you need inspiration or a theme to narrow down your choices.

Colours that appear next to each other will combine harmoniously and easily; colours that are opposite each other on the wheel will jump about and make a noise and give the most intense contrasts, for example blue and orange, or purple and yellow.

Below are some of my favourite colour combinations. All of them together might be too much, but for inspiration you could pick out two or three colours that appear next to each other in the list, such as purple, pink and black, or black, red and acid green.

Grey
Rue (*Ruta graveolens*) – watch out for sap
Perovskia 'Blue Spire'
Hosta (Tardiana Group) 'Hadspen Blue'
Western mugwort 'Silver Queen' (*Artemisia ludoviciana* 'Silver Queen')

Purple
Salvia x *superba*
Round-headed garlic (*Allium sphaerocephalon*)
Smoke bush (*Cotinus coggygria* 'Royal Purple')

Pink
Armenian cranesbill (*Geranium psilostemon*)

Bloody cranesbill (*Geranium sanguineum*)
Bowden Cornish lily (*Nerine bowdenii*)
Purple coneflower (*Echinacea purpurea*)

Black
Phormium 'Platt's Black'
Black grass (*Ophiopogon planiscapus* 'Nigrescens')
Black tulip (*Tulipa* 'Black Parrot')
Ajuga reptans 'Atropurpurea' (not quite black, but very dark purple)

Red
Rosa 'Geranium' *Moyesii* hybrid
Tulipa 'Red Shine'
Day lily (*Hemerocallis* 'Stafford')
Bergamot 'Cambridge Scarlet' (*Monarda* 'Cambridge Scarlet')
Montbretia (*Crocosmia* 'Lucifer')

Acid green
Many-coloured spurge (*Euphorbia polychroma*)
Lady's mantle (*Alchemilla mollis*)
Schilling spurge (*Euphorbia schillingii*)

Medium.05

Rendered Walls

Paula Ryan
Crouch End, London, 2005

Walls need to have a reason for being in a garden to avoid them looking out of place, says designer Paula Ryan, who has made low, freestanding walls something of a trademark, and uses them with skill to define, divide, hide and more.

The garden here is quite long, and one of the primary purposes of the walls is to widen it out and form punctuation marks as the eye travels the length of the garden. 'The client was very keen to have a lawn and the path to the left of it was making something of a runway. Your eye went straight to the back without stopping. But the walls give horizontal lines to the garden and stop your eye from travelling straight down,' says Paula.

The walls define different areas, and veil some parts so that, moving down the garden, more of it is discovered – you do not see it in one fell swoop. At the bottom, the same type of wall are used again, this time to hide a huge shed that would otherwise have been the main focal point of the garden.

The clients also wanted a sitting area at the rear that would catch the evening sun and, if this area had been formed with just the existing boundaries, it would have felt out on a limb. The new walls enclose and, at the same time, anchor the area so that it still feels like part of the garden.

Designer's tip Before designing your garden, look to see where the evening sun is in the summer. Evenings are often the time when people want to sit in the garden, and it is good to put a seating area or even just a bench to catch the last rays.

Designer's tip Paula tells the story of a garden she did using beautifully placed walls to divide up a small space. The client hated it. Paula could not work out why – she had done a design and a sketch of the garden, and the garden had been built to these plans. The problem was that the client, a lady of just 1.5 metres (5 feet) tall, felt completely overwhelmed by the walls. This was resolved by taking down the height. The right dimensions for the walls will not only be defined by the garden, but also by the users.

So what appears to be a simple design is carefully and cleverly thought out. Because each wall fulfils a purpose, none looks out of place and all work together to bring coherence to the garden.

The design skill is obvious. Some of the walls have openings in them – imagine the design with solid walls and it is evident that they would overpower the look of the garden. The openings act as 'windows', offering glimpses through to planting and greenery. This works particularly well for the wall next to the terrace, which is just the right height to put a drink on, to lean on and to look out across the garden. A solid wall of this height would have been forbidding and would have made the terrace very enclosed.

By putting gaps in the walls, Paula has deconstructed them to simple shapes, long white horizontals that float across the garden. The shapes are then repeated with the long white path down the garden and three white uprights on the terrace.

The walls also act as the backdrop for a wonderful modern water feature. Though perhaps an oversimplification, modern water features can be divided into those that use metal, with water running down various metallic curves and balls, and those that use sheets of water dropping

DESIGN BRIEF
• Link with the new extension
• A lawn
• Be practical

FEATURES
• Rendered and painted walls
• Water feature
• Sitting area at rear

from a reservoir. This feature belongs in the latter category.

To get a good wall of water you need a flat horizontal lip for the water to fall over, and behind this a reservoir that fills up to give an even flow of water over the lip. Freestanding walls go with this type of water feature like love and marriage. From a practical point of view, it is easy to get behind the wall for the mechanics and have space for the reservoir of water. And you do not have to worry about any leaks causing damp in a house or boundary wall. The strong horizontal and vertical lines of the water feature here perfectly reflect the lines of the walls. A hole in the wall behind means you can look through the sheet of water to planting, rather than a flat surface.

The walls, then, are the major feature of this garden. They give structure, divert the eye, provide interest and also work for the garden in a number of practical ways.

Because of this strong framework, the planting can be much looser than otherwise. Without the walls, it would look too unstructured. As it is, it provides a free-flowing foil to the crisp lines of the walls. Soft grasses like Mexican feather grass (*Stipa tenuissima*), meadow rue (*Thalictrum aquilegiifolium*), fennel and achilleas are colourful and exuberant, and their shapes play against the flat planes of the painted walls.

One of the major influences on this garden is one that, though not immediately obvious, would certainly be missed were it absent. There are three tall trees – two yews and a pittosporum – which really make the garden. They give a height and a canopy to the space, filtering the light and imbuing the new design with a stability it would not otherwise have.

Designer's tip Never rush into removing trees; they cannot be put back (and they may have a tree preservation order on them). If trees are taking up too much space, one way to retain the benefits of them, but clear more ground space, is to raise the canopy by cutting off the lower branches, which has been done here to great effect.

Next to the house is a beautiful modern terrace. Its floor surface is smooth concrete held between beige granite. Just to show that not everything runs smoothly in the world of the garden designer, the in-situ concrete here proved particularly problematic. Concrete needs to be laid in dry weather; given the climate in the UK, this can be a major problem. Also, the mix needs to be exactly the same for each pouring, or the finished colour will change. And cats are simply just not welcome when you have got fresh concrete on the ground. Looking at the finished result here, you would be completely unaware of the turbulent history of this piece of land.

Simple, but beautiful, is the trelliswork next to the terrace, where three screens of horizontal slats of pine are held between bold white columns.

The overall design for this garden had to reflect a very modern new interior that was, as Paula says, 'so crisp and white we had to link this in with the garden'. By using the white walls, the design has taken that crispness into the garden and made a usable and useful space. As a result, there was no need to be minimalist in the planting, and it is this contrast of airy planting with the stark white structure of the walls that brings the garden to life.

BELOW LEFT: On the terrace, sharply clipped box bushes (*Buxus sempervirens*) provide geometric shapes.

BELOW MIDDLE: The rendered walls act as vases for the bold planting.

OPPOSITE: The rendered walls of the new extension fit perfectly with the clean, modern look of the garden.

ABOVE: Looking down the garden, the horizontal lines of the walls widen its appearance and mitigate the effects of the long path to the side.

LEFT: The light-coloured walls and the limestone flooring give a bright, almost Mediterranean, feel to the terrace.

BELOW: Walls are useful for many things.

ABOVE: A gap in the wall takes the weight out of it and is used as a shelf for candles.

Walls

Freestanding walls are being used more and more often in garden design, and it is easy to see why. They are practical and durable, and the rendered, painted examples in modern gardens give them a stylish feel.

Walls can be used for many different purposes:

- *For dividing up a space.* Like any screen, walls can be used to form actual or implied boundaries to divide up areas.
- *To create interest.* Often walls are used like flats on a stage to punctuate the scene as it moves away from the eye.
- *For structure.* Walls can provide very strong horizontal and vertical lines to the garden.
- *For concealing.* Solid and potentially tall, walls are great for completely masking the unsightly and unwanted.
- *As seating.* Walls can hold seats. The horizontal line of modern inbuilt seating looks beautifully sculptural against a flat plane. Placed at the right height, walls can also make extra, uncluttered seating or, if higher, a bar to lean against, look over and contemplate the world.
- *As a planting backdrop.* The colour of the wall is important for this. There are no rules, and part of the fun is experimenting with colour, but contrasts are always

a good place to start. If the wall is light coloured, try brightly coloured plants, and vice versa.
- *For shadow play.* Whether you use sunlight or uplighters, bold planting or unstructured, the effects of shadow play on the flat surface of a wall is magical.
- *To display.* In this garden, the wall provides the perfect surround to a modern water feature, but walls can also be used to define and 'hold' sculpture in the garden.
- *For contrast.* This is where walls come into their own. The starkness and purity of their lines play so well in a garden setting where they can be placed against exuberant or architectural planting.

Wall design

Walls do not have to form flat, regular planes.

Cut-outs
In this garden, the holes are rectangles. But you could also use circular, oval or freeform holes and gaps. These will lighten the wall and can act as viewing holes or places through which to shine lights, or simply look good.

Niches
The holes do not have to go all the way through the wall. Niches can be created for sitting or for placing sculpture, or just painted a different colour.

Curves
Walls can curve, snake about or form almost complete circles to enclose an area.

Surface
Most of the walls in this book are rendered and painted. This gives a clean, modern canvas, but be careful what capping you use along the top – use the wrong capping and it can look awful. To avoid the 'hacienda' look and get a really clean line, avoid using anything even remotely rustic, including bricks. Only use the sleekest stone, or avoid the issue altogether and use beading at the edges instead.

Columns
Walls do not have to be long. Tall columns can be used to define an area and provide a strong, repeated pattern.

Practical matters
- Walls may need planning permission; it is best to ask first.
- Rendered and painted walls will need regular maintenance.
- Walls are a major construction in a garden and can cause huge damage if built incorrectly. If in doubt, get specialist advice.

Large

L Introduction

In large gardens there is space to run about and room to create surprises, it is not quite so necessary to use all of the garden, and the design can be looser, using less geometric shapes. But enclosure and division become more important in a larger space, as without them a garden of this size can look like a playing field and feel uncomfortable. The enclosed areas can be created and used for different purposes: for vegetables, to make a courtyard garden or, in the case of the Concrete Terrace garden, simply to break up a large area to give it a more pleasant feel. Each enclosure needs to have good proportions, and the space it creates needs to feel right and be right for its purpose. But new areas also need to fit in with the rest of the garden. In the Country Swirls garden, the space is left largely open, though a circular inner room is implied by the large planted bed that surrounds it. This curving central space would not be so at home in its surroundings had the overall proportions of the garden not also been changed. The ground plan is almost square, but it has been formed into a sweeping spiral by the beds enclosed within the garden, which is made much softer and more inviting as a result.

So spatial division is quite complex, and movement through the spaces it creates is also an important part of the design. However, though paths and walkways are therefore major elements of any garden, they are often – even by garden designers – put in as an afterthought. They are important because they define how a garden is experienced. Think of any great garden, and you can see how the designer has exploited the knowledge of how the users of the garden will move around it.

Paths are fundamental to the unfolding ambience of a garden. Designers know that you will come out of a dark enclosed area into the light, they know that by widening the path at a certain point it will cause you to pause and, when you do, you will have a certain view or focal point. They know that you will hear the sound of water before you see the fountain, and that this will excite your curiosity and draw you onwards. Integral to a design, paths also form patterns and structure, by joining and dividing areas. And at a more practical level, they can provide all-weather walkways to get around the garden, and allow access for maintenance.

ABOVE RIGHT: The apparent proportions of the Country Swirls garden have been changed by creating an inner 'room' surrounded by planted beds.

RIGHT: Paths can be more than simply a way to get from A to B. Here they form the pattern and structure of the garden.

Path design

- As a practical first step, mark on a ground plan all of the features that need access by way of a hard surface: house doors, climbing frames, gates, garages and outbuildings.
- Major routes can be wider, at least a metre (3.2 feet) wide, to allow two people to walk side by side.
- You can manipulate how people will walk around the garden: for example, a meandering path will encourage them to slow down, whereas a narrow straight path will encourage them to speed up.
- The character of the path will be partly determined by its shape. A straight path will tend to be formal and jump out as a feature of the design. Curving paths tend to be natural, they may follow the contours of the landscape, and tend not to impose themselves on the design.

Choosing a surface

Paths can be of soft materials like gravel, decking or old brick, very natural materials like chipped bark or log slices or, at the other extreme, very defined sharp materials such as polished concrete or marble. Things to bear in mind when deciding which material to use for paths or walkways include:

- The style of the house and the garden – a concrete path will jar against an old cottage. Similarly, wood chips will not look good in a very slick modern garden.
- Using local materials – fitting in with the vernacular will always help hard landscaping look right in a garden.
- The purpose of the path – how heavy will the traffic along it be? Will people walk on it with bare feet? Will small children see gravel or bark-chip paths as sandpits?
- Cost – aggregates and bark chip tend to be the cheapest materials, and are less labour-intensive to lay.

Designer's tip Lines of desire are something to consider, especially if you have children. For example, if a swing is positioned a little way off from the back door, a child's line of desire will be a straight line between the two. As children (and sometimes adults) tend to take the route of least resistance, if it is easier to trample on a flowerbed than to go around it, they probably will. You can either give in and put a path there instead, or make it more difficult to travel this straight route by planting large shrubs. However, this is more tricky where there are lines of desire across a lawn, where you cannot put up barriers and the grass will become worn if the same line is taken each time. In this case, stepping stones across the lawn will help.

Large.01

Country Swirls
Julie Toll
Essex, 2002–03

The cues for this garden have been taken from the gentle hills, fields, hedgerows and meadows of the surrounding countryside. The designer, Julie Toll, says: 'A major part of the brief was that the garden should belong to the countryside that borders the garden on two sides.'

And this she has done. The garden previously sloped down to a retaining wall right next to the house, creating an enclosed and claustrophobic feeling. It has been resculpted, reworked and transformed. Julie has worked with the slope of the land, but has gently moulded it into a beautiful and usable space. It is, as ever, amazing how much work and thought goes into getting a garden to look natural.

The main work came in taking back the land, away from the house, and creating a swirling pattern for the beds that culminates in a grassy dip at the centre of the garden. Major earthworks like this have some potential hazards: for example, altering ground levels interferes with natural drainage patterns, and water will collect at the bottom of any dips you make. Julie managed to get around this problem using land drains that feed off into surrounding ditches.

Designer's tip If you are creating a grassy bank or dip, think about how the grass will be cut. An ordinary mower can cope with a slight incline, but if it is too steep you will need to use a Flymow or strimmer, and it can be hard work to keep it looking good.

The dip here has only a very slight slope, so it is easy to maintain, and it also fits nicely with the easy, natural feel of the garden. A steep dip would have yelled 'I've been designed', and made too much of a statement.

What does make a statement, though, is a gleaming stainless-steel water feature at the lowest point of the dip, which provides an upright accent and a strong contrast with the country look all around. The water feature is also the main focal point of the garden and has been placed here, off to the side, for very good reason. The garden is wider than it is long, and the entrance and main views into it are to the side. Look straight ahead from here and you ignore most of the garden, so the focal point draws the eye to the side, opens up the diagonal view and increases the feeling of space.

Around the edges of the swirling lawn are deep planted beds filled with wonderful perennials and shrubs. 'We wanted natural planting, a cross between wild and cultivated, something that looked like an overgrown meadow.' Julie has designed the beds to reach a colourful peak at the end of summer, which is something the clients were very keen on – they did not want a garden that looked spent by the end of July.

The plants are laid out in an intricate and inspired matrix. It is haphazard, but done with such deftness and expertise that it works. Patterns and connections are made, but nothing is put in clumps. 'I like to see what plants look like with each other. Often single plants look good together where, if they were in threes or fives, they would look wrong,' says Julie. Avoiding groups and blocks gives such a delicacy to the structure that it looks light and natural. This is a difficult look to get right, requiring skill, knowledge and artistry, but the result is spectacular.

DESIGN BRIEF
• Fit with the surrounding countryside
• Mixture of the natural and controlled
• Not necessarily low maintenance

FEATURES
• Swirling, dipping lawn
• Green oak steps
• Stainless-steel water feature

The garden changes enormously through the seasons. In the spring and early summer it is bursting with potential in the lead up to its full glory at the end of summer, and the perennials used look good well into the winter. Soft grasses like *Deschampsia cespitosa* 'Goldschleier' provide a foil for the strong forms of persicaria (*Persicaria amplexicaulis* 'Firetail'). Some plants have good form that lasts well into the winter, like the four different types of Miscanthus (*Miscanthus sinensis* 'Flamingo', *M.s.* 'Kleine Silberspinne', *M.s.* 'Malepartus' and *M. s.* 'Morning Light') and others, like the coneflower (*Echinacea purpurea* 'Magnus'), have seed heads that will stay standing.

Designer's tip In amongst the perennials are carefully placed large box bushes (*Buxus sempervirens*), clipped into balls, that are almost unnoticeable in summer but in winter give structure to the beds.

The lines of the garden swirl out from the grassy dip and around to the patio where the land previously fell precipitously down to the house. The fall has been softened and taken away from the house to open up the patio and give a better view from within. Broad, deep steps are in green oak and grass. The oak was intended to give some structure, but the idea was to have organic steps, to fit with the softness of the garden. The green oak may twist and split, but, as Julie says: 'We didn't want a perfect look, and green oak gives a natural look that blends in with the garden.'

Designer's tip Using grass on steps will work if the steps are wide, because people will take a different path up or down them each time. If the steps are narrow, the grass will quickly become worn.

Similarly, on the patio a mix of natural materials has been used that, with age, will fit in with their surrounds. Mixing stone, brick, gravel and planting pockets gives a soft structure to what otherwise could have been an overpowering amount of hard landscaping. A central area of York stone has been reserved for a large oak table and chairs, surrounded by pockets of low-growing plants.

Also on the patio is a small Wendy house for the children, which can be removed in a few years when they grow out of it. Otherwise, there is not anything overtly for children in this design. Toys come and go over the years, and the children make their own games, as children always do. The change in levels and secret areas created naturally in the garden provide adventure for them. 'I think the main thing,' says Julie, 'is that the garden isn't too fussy; it doesn't matter if the children pick flowers or bump into things.' This also fits in with the philosophy of this garden. It is a very gentle, natural garden, and its elements flow easily. And it has that elusive attribute sought by every garden designer: it looks like it is meant to be here.

LEFT: Curving steps are planted on either side with herbs.

OPPOSITE TOP: The soft swirling shapes of the garden blend in with the country feel of the house and surrounding countryside.

OPPOSITE BOTTOM: Although pleasing for adults, at the same time the garden, with its many hiding places, has much of interest for children.

ABOVE: Just providing a child-sized place to sit like this tent, from Wingreen, is enough to make a garden for children.

LEFT: Miscanthus and cotinus come into their own in late summer and autumn to catch the lower, golden sun.

OPPOSITE: The water feature is the focal point of the grassy dip.

ABOVE: In late summer, the russet and gold tones of the planting are just beginning to reach their peak.

LEFT AND BELOW: The sandpit is hidden away around the corner and out of sight, and is great for children up to the ages of seven or eight.

ABOVE: Lavender pekins are pretty, well-behaved bantams and make ideal family pets.

Keeping chickens

Chickens are a great addition to a family garden, producing organic eggs, organic fertiliser and a nice warm fuzzy feeling when you see them wandering around your garden. They are great, low-maintenance pets. They need letting out in the morning and closing up at night, and when you check for eggs you need to make sure they have water and food, and these are jobs that are easily done by a child.

Like any pet, chickens will need looking after if you go on holiday. However, because the job is so easy it is not something that a neighbour would usually object to – especially if rewarded with fresh eggs.

If you want to keep chickens, here are a few hints to get going:

- If you do not want to breed them, stick to females unless you want to be woken up early.
- Each chicken lays one egg roughly every other day (fewer in winter), so two or three should provide enough eggs for a family.
- Bantams (small chickens) are very pretty, do not scratch about too fiercely and are generally good with children.
- You will need a house for your chickens, for shelter and to protect against foxes and vermin. If you are new to chickens, I would buy the house ready-made – I built ours and made a couple of silly mistakes.
- It is a good idea to have a movable house, small enough to lift and tip out for cleaning.

- If the chickens are going to roam about in the daytime, you will not need a protected outside area. But if you are going to be late home or away for a day or so, it is worth having something you can put up where they can get outside but be safe.
- You can get big sacks of specialist feed for chickens that will last for a long time. This can go in a feeder – you fill it up and it falls down as the chickens eat it. Water dispensers that work in a similar way are also available.

Large.02

Grass Sculpture
Fiona and Chris Royffe
Yorkshire, 1995–2005

This garden was formed when a large country house was divided up into separate residences. The building to which it belongs used to house the old butler's quarters and stables and is at the side of the main building, which means the garden wraps around it and has interesting outbuildings and yards.

The different areas have been added to, to create a garden of distinct yet interlinking 'rooms', all of which have their own ambience but are not cut off from each other. Just outside the house is the first of the rooms – a shady court-yard with a high canopy to one side to keep the rain off the dining table underneath.

Designer's tip The covered seating area is beautifully light – corrugated plastic above allows sunlight in, but keeps the rain off. Though not the prettiest material, it does the job very well. Here it has been placed well above eye level so that you do not notice the plastic.

Around to the side is a stableyard, divided off with pleached hornbeams (*Carpinus betulus*). While these form a boundary, they still allow views both in and out of this area.

The garden rises up to incorporate dry beds and sloping lawn as it turns the corner from the stableyard round to the back of the house. The ground level was raised and dipped to create interest and reinforce the design. When Fiona and Chris Royffe, from garden design firm Plants By Design, moved in here nearly a decade ago, the ground was flat and, apart from some very mature trees, there was little else in the garden.

Chris explains: 'Part of the challenge was to relate the new garden to its surrounds, but also to maintain privacy within.' He has achieved this with a very structured design,

with links back to the formal gardens of great country houses yet enclosed using hedges and by changing the lie of the land. The land sculpting has also been used to give high platforms from which to view the surrounding countryside of the estate through carefully framed in openings in the hedges. At the rear of the garden is what Chris calls a 'rampart', a raised berm of grassy soil that further enhances the feeling of seclusion.

Though the garden is not large, the number of interlinking spaces gives a real feeling of discovery as you move through it, which can be enjoyed by both children and adults. Tiny hidden pathways are scattered throughout to invite the intrepid to explore. As Chris explains: 'The paths through the planting work for children and for adults. We wanted to give a different experience of the planting; we wanted people to be able to get right in the middle of it rather than just viewing it from the sides.'

Designer's tip Children love the grassy banks and small precipices formed by the land sculpting here.

The couple's children have now left home, and the garden has moved on with the family. 'The garden has matured with the family. Over the years the structure has become more apparent and we've taken out temporary features that gave it impact initially.'

Curving yew hedges (*Taxus baccata*) are now prominent and used to divide up the garden and provide horizontal accents. These were all in Chris's original design, which he did shortly after the couple moved in, but are only now

DESIGN BRIEF
- A separate garden within a larger country estate
- Structure and seating areas
- Make the most of views around the garden

FEATURES
- Grass sculpture
- Covered seating area
- Yew hedges

taking centre stage in the garden.

Parking was previously right in front of the house, and the Royffes wanted to move the cars back and screen them. They also wanted to create a real entrance to the garden. This has been achieved by making a vista down from the front door and enclosing the front garden with beech hedges (*Fagus sylvatica*). The vista is marked by groups of white-stemmed silver birch trees (*Betula utilis var. jacquemontii*) that lead the eye down to the countryside. The enclosed front garden has a chequerboard of sculpted box bushes (*Buxus sempervirens*) set in gravel to give formality to the shady area.

ABOVE: Pleached hornbeams (*Carpinus betulus*) suggest a divide between the stableyard and the rest of the garden.

LEFT: Phormiums, ferns and euphorbias give interesting textures in a shady corner.

OPPOSITE: The garden sweeps up and around from the courtyard before opening out to lawn.

TOP: In the vegetable area, box (*Buxus sempervirens*) pyramids help to give structure in the summer and provide greenery in the winter.

ABOVE: Throughout the garden, secret paths sneak behind hedges and through flowerbeds – drawing in both adults and children.

RIGHT: Strong lines of hedges and tree stems contrast with the diaphanous planting.

LEFT: A grassy avenue leads to the front door, framed by white-barked silver birch trees (*Betula utilis var. jacquemontii*).
RIGHT: With a nod to the grand traditions of the country house, the geometric pattern of box (*Buxus sempervirens*) cubes formalises the gravelled front entrance.

Front gardens

The front garden of this house has been turned into something of a statement. It announces strongly to the world: 'Here we are – this is the front door.' This was necessary because the grander front entrance to the attached historic building could overshadow that of the more modest residence. But, in general, front gardens are not seen as a priority in design; they don't get a lot of use, so the temptation is to just let them be. However, it is worth putting a little effort in to them to announce to the world where you are and who you are.

Design
• Front gardens are often small spaces and, because they are in full view, not necessarily places you would want to relax in. So they often have a mainly decorative function, the only practicality being getting people from the road to the front door. Even this consideration can cause problems. A straight path tends not to look good, and a curved path can be a pain every time you want to get to the front door.
• A solution can be to make a less distinct path. Use hard-landscaping materials over a wide and, possibly, curving area, but the path taken can be as straight as you like.

• Another element in the design is to make it clear where the front door is. The path, however wide, should point the visitor in the right direction.

Style
• In front gardens, the architecture tends to be dominant – not just the architecture of your own house, but that of the surrounding houses too. Though you can fight against it, going with the style of the street and the houses often works best. In a row of cottages, a stainless-steel minimalist creation could work, but probably will not.

Car parking
• Even the tiniest front gardens are being turned into parking spaces, as on-street parking becomes more restricted. I feel I ought to point out that it is bad for the environment and for the look of the place, but I can understand why people do it.
• If there is room, try not to let the car dominate the approach to the house or the view from it. Evergreen planting is good for screening without adding to the built environment.
• Gravel is good for parking, as it is soft. A gravel surface can look like a garden when nothing is parked on it, and planting pockets can be included in areas not used by cars

to soften the look. If space is really tight, low plants can be put in between where the car wheels will stand.
• Paving for cars needs to be able to take the weight of vehicles. Large paving stones are inflexible and likely to crack under the weight. Cobbles, setts and gravel are ideal, and a mix of materials will add interest and give subtle clues for directing people to the front door.

Safety and security
• Anyone approaching doors or windows should, if possible, be visible from the street. This goes against our natural need for privacy, but is wise and will also light up the house.
• Gravel on the ground will crunch underfoot and help reveal anyone approaching the house.
• A movement-sensitive security light is also a good idea.
• If possible, make sure children do not play in, and do not have access to, areas where cars reverse.

Large.03

Concrete Terrace

Andrew Wilson
Surrey, 2002

This garden should not work. For a start, there are the uncompromising proportions. The space is 65 x 15 metres (213 x 49 feet) – a huge expanse to be filled. Then there is the brief: rather than dividing up the space, it was to be opened up so that the view beyond can be seen from the house. And finally, the design solution: concrete. But despite all this, what designer Andrew Wilson has achieved is a bold and beautiful garden that gives a peaceful and beautiful space within which to entertain.

The impetus for doing the work came from a new extension, a family room on the side of the house. The extension is built around an existing birch tree, which now grows up through its roof, and has huge, curving glass windows. Around to the side, the garden rises up under tall pine trees. It was clear that little would grow here, so the area has been landscaped with gravel and steps. From this point, the rest of the garden cascades around the house, and it is along the back of the house where the main design work was necessary.

The first thing to realise here is the scale. The terrace just goes on and on. 'To feel comfortable in the space, it needed to be broken up, but we didn't want to remove the open views nor the ability to look along the terrace,' says Andrew. This seemingly insurmountable design problem was neatly resolved by the ingenious use of walls set at right angles to the house. At different heights and with breaks in them, the walls enclose, yet at the same time allow views down the terrace. And of course, set at right angles to the house, they do not impede the views out. As Andrew says, the walls do not divide, but do 'give a spatial structure to the area'.

The gaps in the walls also let in shafts of light that cut through the planting, making an interesting play of light and shade. And the walls themselves have a further benefit, acting as light fittings. Lights shine against them at night so that they gently glow in the dark.

The walls are made of concrete blocks and rendered with coloured concrete. The colour, 'Shadow slate', was chosen to complement the flooring. Along the top they have a coping of Marshall's conservation curb, to match the steps that are finished in the same material. On the floor are the poured-concrete slabs, again of dyed concrete. This time the colour is 'French slate'. But why use concrete? 'The concrete render on the walls and poured concrete slabs on the floor give a semi-industrial look to the project and keep the clean lines in a way that other materials would not,' says Andrew. Concrete is also a great solution for dealing with the large size of the floor area, where choice of flooring is often difficult. Most slabs are less than 1.5 metres (5 feet) square, which would give a busy, broken feel to the space. Poured concrete allows blocks of 3 metres (10 feet) and more, which work in harmony with the size of the area. Between the slabs is granite gravel – without this the area would be too bland and flat – which provides a juxtaposition of texture that lifts the area.

There is no formula for the exact positioning of the walls, their heights and where to position the gaps. It is pure artistry. Though there is a balance and rhythm to the spacing, it is not an exact pattern but an accomplished harmony of water, plants and hard materials.

Water is central to the design; a long infinity pool reaches the edge of the terrace and drops off the edge into a lower pool. Contractor Mark Gregory had to get this 13-metre (43-foot) edge absolutely level. More than a millimetre (0.03 inches) out, and the fine lip of water would be broken.

DESIGN BRIEF
- Something different and architectural
- Semi-industrial feel to fit with new extension
- Maintain views out to the garden
- Large seating area for entertaining

FEATURES
- Concrete rendered walls
- Poured concrete floor
- Infinity pool

Andrew points out that the film of water running over the edge needed to be very thin: 'It was quite difficult to get the water to move without it making a noise or causing too many ripples, which would lose the reflective quality. But I wanted this razor-sharp edge on the horizon of the terrace.' The pool is lined with black fibreglass to maximise the reflections.

Beyond the inspired design idea of the walls, contrasts are what make this garden work. The walls cut at the light and allow contrasts of light and shade. And their heaviness is contradicted as they appear to float on the water they are juxtaposed with. In the planting, too, sharp contrasts of form and texture bring the scheme to life. Bold architectural planting like Spanish dagger (*Yucca gloriosa*) and the line of privet lollipops (*Ligustrum delavayanum*) give strong definition, while soft grasses, such as tussock (*Deschampsia cespitosa* 'Goldtau'), blur in the breeze. Softness also comes from the herbaceous plantings of sage (*Salvia* x *sylvestris* 'Mainacht') and hardy geranium (*Geranium* 'Johnson's Blue').

Light and shade, water and concrete, strong and airy planting. Contrasts work best between extremes, and to achieve a result like this you need to be brave. However, the results, as here, can be stunning.

ABOVE: Water flows seamlessly over the edge of the infinity pool.

LEFT: The concrete render on the walls, though it is a different colour, complements the poured concrete on the ground.

OPPOSITE: At different heights, the walls divide without enclosing and so do not become overpowering.

ABOVE: The new fibreglass-and-glass extension wraps around the corner of the house and encloses a large silver birch tree within its structure.

RIGHT: Alliums provide seasonal colour and add to the blue-and-silver theme of the planting and concrete.

ABOVE: A concrete rendered wall with a kerbstone along the top.

Concrete

Speaking to Mark Gregory, the contractor who worked on this garden, you begin to realise there is more to concrete than meets the eye. It is an ancient substance that was known to the Romans, which has been resoundingly out of fashion since the 1960s. But in design circles it is making a comeback. The good news about concrete is that it is, as Mark says, 'very creative and you can get interesting sizes and shapes'. Richard Day of the Concrete Society lists the following pros and cons when using concrete:

Pros
- Concrete can be moulded to wonderful shapes that you just cannot get with other materials.
- It can be polished. This is when the concrete is poured and sets, but later a thin layer is ground off to reveal the aggregates in a very smooth surface.
- Things can be laid in it, including steel strips to create patterns and define areas.

- Colouring can be achieved by pouring pigment into fresh concrete before it is laid, or by using a coloured surface hardener, which is added after pouring but before the mix has hardened (gone off). The former gives a muted colour, the latter a more intense colour.

Cons
- Handling and mixing need to be done with care. Concrete is strongly alkaline and can cause dermatitis. Mixing on site is usually the best option for a relatively small job in a garden, but it is easy to get the mix wrong. Often there is not enough cement and too much water, which leaves a surface that is vulnerable to the weather.
- Concrete on the ground needs a strong sub-base. It is very strong in compression, but weak in tension, and if the sub-base is not even it will crack.
- Formwork needs to be appropriate, and this is especially important on upright structures. Concrete is formed with water, so is very heavy and will crack formwork that is not robust enough. For slabs, the formwork needs to be dead straight, which can mean you have to spend money on high-quality wood.
- Slabs larger than 4 square metres (43 square feet) are prone to cracking when the concrete shrinks, so you may need to limit the size of blocks, and keep to square shapes, to prevent this.

Large.04

Linking Rooms
Debbie Roberts and Ian Smith
Surrey, 1998

How far to enclose? How much to divide up a space? These are major considerations at the beginning of the design process. The benefits of dividing up a space are many: you can create interest, areas to discover and better proportions in the garden. Any garden designer will tell you exactly this. But in your own garden, if the existing space is flat and open, this is quite a brave thing to commit to. Instead of having wonderful open space you will, apparently, draw in the boundaries and close off the long views.

This garden was originally a large area of lawn sweeping around the house with little of interest. However, though it has now been divided up into very distinct areas, its two central lawns maintain the feeling of space and openness. There are hidden walkways, sheltered sitting areas, and hedges to enclose. Done well, this screening and dividing adds a feeling of discovery to the garden and there is interest and intimacy to be found in all of the areas.

Debbie Roberts, of Acres Wild, the design team that worked on this garden, sees the design 'as a series of interlocking rooms, each with its own atmosphere'. The largest of the areas is formed by the two lawns at the centre of the garden, which are separated by steps and a paved seating area. The steps provide elegance and formality to the lawn space and break up what other-wise have been a very large expanse of grass.

The lawns, along with the other areas of the garden, have very defined structures to provide geometric shapes. Debbie calls this 'controlled structure'. Next to this, however, she uses loose, informal planting schemes. Around the lawn areas, miscanthus (*Miscanthus sinensis*) and smoke bush (*Cotinus coggygria*) give height, while beneath, hot-coloured perennials like bright-pink mullein (*Lychnis coronaria*) and red crocosmia (*Crocosmia* 'Lucifer') brighten up the scheme.

The framework is formal, but rather than being imposed on the landscape it relates to its setting: 'We always look very closely at the land forms that are there and work with them to create the design.' Here the land sloped down slightly and this has been used to create the two levels to the lawns with steps between.

Designer's tip In a contained space, let the changes in level happen under the planting and make sure the lawn is absolutely flat. This will look more elegant and be easier to mow. It will also help to relate the lawn space to other flat surfaces such as the terrace.

Around to the rear of the house is a covered loggia, built especially for outdoor eating. This is a perfect example of an indoor–outdoor area. It looks out over its own garden, a courtyard with a wonderful geometric water feature running its length. The feeling here is Mediterranean and the planting reflects this: lavenders, herbs and cynara give a sunny, scented atmosphere. The flooring is made of gravel, terracotta and patterns of cobbles set in concrete.

The formal areas of the garden are punctuated with carefully placed containers. On either side of the courtyard, these reinforce its symmetry. Around the house, as each area moves through to the next, twin containers mark the entrances. Planted with formal architectural plants, like box (*Buxus sempervirens*) and various phormiums, these help define the structure of the garden.

DESIGN BRIEF
- Create separate, but linked, spaces
- Outside eating area
- A garden that evolves

FEATURES
- Loggia with courtyard
- Naturalistic stream
- Containers

Away from the house, the garden becomes less formal and a natural-looking stream with a woodland walk has been incorporated at the far end.

Designer's tip To get a stream to look natural, place it away from the house and conceal it so that it is not on show. Slope the ground down to the stream and make sure there is lots of planting around. What you are doing is mimicking nature: a natural stream would flow along the lowest point in the garden and there would be lots of planting to make the most of the moisture in the stream.

The stream is a more recent addition to this garden. At the time of the original design, the children were still small and a stream would have been a safety risk. The designers did, however, build it into their initial plan, so that, as the years went on, what was a dry river bed could be filled with water. Similarly, a raised play area has now been commandeered for an evening 'G&T area'. This satisfied the clients' brief for a family garden that would be adaptable and evolve as the children grew up.

'Understanding clients' needs,' says Debbie, 'is an essential part of the design process. We need to know what they want to use the garden for and how their needs will develop.' The clients wanted different rooms in their garden, areas with distinct characters and feels, and the design here creates an ambience that changes as you move around the garden. From the open, elegant formality of the lawns, you move on to the enclosed scented courtyard, and the feeling changes again as you enter the woodland walk by the stream.

Dividing up the garden has allowed these separate areas to be created; they have been placed around the open space of the lawn and related to their surroundings. The courtyard leads off the loggia, and the stream has been placed against a backdrop of mature trees that border the garden. Without division, this design would not have been possible.

ABOVE: The courtyard to the loggia includes this beautiful, formal water feature.

LEFT: Bold stands of miscanthus and alchemilla give a softness to contrast with the structured design.

OPPOSITE: The two lawns are divided by steps and a paved seating area.

OVERLEAF: The loggia provides a wonderful outdoor eating area overlooking its own courtyard.

LEFT: Bold seasonal planting works well in large containers.
RIGHT: Box (*Buxus sempervirens*) provides a wonderful, year-round sculptural effect.

Containers

Plant pots have come a long way in recent years. It is no longer a case of just terracotta, PVC or wood. Fibreglass and metal containers are now making inroads, and you can often find them in your local garden centre.

Using containers means that you have just a nice, bite-sized chunk of gardening to do – something you can feel comfortable with and not burdened by. The only time they might be a nuisance is in high summer, when they may need watering every day. Using large containers and perhaps using an automatic watering system will help with this.

Containers also provide great ornament to a garden, and colour that can change to suit your mood or alongside the seasons. I have to admit I am a bit of a puritan when it comes to containers: one type of plant in each, and probably one type of plant for all, and if you want to play safe go for strong shapes rather than fluffy flowers. This may seem a little boring, but this way you will get a much more modern, architectural look to the scheme. If you are using just one plant, the main thing is that it should be in proportion to the container.

The following plants are all suitable for containers:

Ophiopogon
This evergreen grass-like plant works well in window boxes. The black variety (*Ophiopogon planiscapus* 'Nigrescens') is the most common, but shades of green and grey are also available.

Stonecrop 'Ruby Glow' (*Sedum* 'Ruby Glow')
With purple leaves, this will flop over the sides and work with taller grey containers. It prefers sun and will die down in winter.

Box (*Buxus sempervirens*)
This can be cut to any size, into balls, cones or columns. Squared off it looks good in tall, straight-sided containers.

Phormium tenax 'Purpureum Group'
This can get huge, so a big container is best to stop a top-heavy appearance. It is not completely hardy, and prefers full sun.

Black bamboo (*Phyllostachys nigra*)
Their upright habit makes these plants well suited to containers. They are tall, so can form a screen if planted in a long container.

Agapanthus 'Black Pantha'
This tall blue/black flowers on the top of architectural leaves are great for a late-autumn display. It dies down in winter and prefers a sunny spot.

Tulipa 'Red Shine'
Shorter tulips are more likely to make a good mass and not flop all over the place, but some taller ones, like this ruby red one, are known for staying upright.

Big blue lily turf (*Liriope muscari*)
This evergreen grass-like plant has purple flowers in the autumn.

Hosta (Tardiana Group) 'Hadspen Blue'
Hostas are great for containers, and their form works especially well with short, wide-shaped pots. They are only on show in the summer, and you need to keep the slugs out. (Use sharp grit or Vaseline around the top of the pot, but try to avoid using slug pellets.)

Hebe salicifolia
Hebes are evergreen bushes with a good strong shape and flowers during summer. This one is a large variety with particularly nice leaves and white/pink flowers. It prefers sun.

Large.05

City Secrets

Oliver Smith
Mile End, London, 2004

What do you do when you buy a historic townhouse with a traditional garden, but want to inject a Modernist feel into them? There are lots of ways to go about this, but the way it has been done here works extremely well.

It is interesting how the house and garden mirror one another. Each is historically special and needed to keep its own spirit. Any additions had to be sympathetic. The main structure of the Georgian house has been left untouched, the new modern extension sitting gently upon it with due reverence to its historical value – adding to, but not detracting from, it.

Similarly, neither was it an option to run roughshod over the garden and change it completely. But the access to the garden and the way the house and garden worked together needed to be changed. Previously, a single door with a flight of steps down to the garden provided the only access. Now, to cater for modern needs, Oliver Smith, from architectural firm 5th Studio, has created a stunning extension that takes the living space down to the level of the garden. 'The house had no real relationship with the garden, so the extension was designed to open up the house to the garden and integrate the two,' says Oliver. Made largely of glass, the extension hangs lightly on the original house with minimum interference.

The extension has created a dining area with beautiful views out to the garden, which, carefully created by the architects, is symmetrical and modern, with bamboos, liriopes and grasses forming a minimalist planting palette. The rectangular lawn nips in at the end to emphasise its length and, on either side of the nip, huge phormiums form symmetrical sentinels.

The extension sits quite a bit lower than the garden. Normally this is resolved by moving the earth back so that the lower level extends out and into the garden. However, an enormous beech tree that could not be moved meant that this was not possible here, and dictated that the higher level remained quite close to the door. Steps just outside the entrance lead up to the garden, and outside the dining room is a pool that brings the higher level right up to the house. This is a wonderful way around the change in level and has meant that, instead of being a problem, it has been turned into an advantage. The higher level of the pool means you can sit inside on the window seat at the same level as the water outside, looking over the surface of the water into the garden.

Designer's tip Putting the water next to the house like this has another advantage – it is very easy to keep an eye on children playing around the pool.

Stepping-stones across the pool break up its surface and, along the side wall, a step has been created to allow candles to be put alongside the water. The bottom of the pool has been lined with dark slate to maximise reflections.

Beyond the pool is a long container of architectural horsetails and black grass that mark a further step up. Because the dining room is low, these are viewed from the side, which emphasises their sculptural forms.

But over to the side is a hint of what is to come. An old-fashioned pergola covered in climbing roses comes straight to the back door and, down through this, you can just catch glimpses of an old convent garden.

Walking down the garden, under the arches, the history and sense of discovery is palpable, and it is like

DESIGN BRIEF
• Modern garden to mix with old existing garden
• Open up house and garden

FEATURES
• Reflecting pool
• Pergola
• Cloister garden

entering a different world. At the bottom of the path, the garden opens up to the area where nuns once walked and meditated. The paths are worn into ruts and there are still the remains of a cloister to the rear. A formal layout of four beds is arranged around a central water cistern that is carefully set up on a plinth.

Designer's tip In the stonework here, there is a mix of old, and new posing as old. You can buy reclaimed materials, or alternatively age new ones by dousing them in yoghurt or leaving them in long grass for a season.

The planting in the beds is also a mix of old and new, formal and informal. Lollipopped bay trees (*Laurus nobilis*) and upright junipers (*Juniperus scopulorum* 'Skyrocket') give punctuation at the corners of the beds, and low box hedges (*Buxus sempervirens*) around the edges give structure. Inside, the planting is loose and riotous, with lavenders, golden oat grass (*Stipa gigantea*), poppies, nigella and artemisia spilling over the edges. The combination of the formal, the clipped and this loose planting works wonderfully. It is almost like putting flowers in a vase, as their colour and abundance contrasts with the strong lines around their base.

This is one of those gardens that touches you. Whether it is the unexpected nature of coming across the old part, or the sense of history or the sheer peace and quiet that is achieved in the centre of the city – this is a magical garden. And it is the sort of effect that, with some thought, can be achieved in any garden. Though we do not all have an ancient cloister, there are a number of things that can help re-create such a look.

First is the sense of mystery and discovery. This is a secret garden, almost completely concealed. When you happen upon it and it opens up before you, there is a 'wow' factor. Hiding an area of a garden requires a little space, but is quite easy to do with hedges and planting.

The idea is that you turn a corner or take a path and discover something beautiful. Not only is the cloister here hidden, it is also unexpected. Because the rest of the garden is so modern and formal, stumbling across something so different is inspiring. This contrast of styles adds to the effect. It is also a quiet and ordered space that imparts a real sense of well-being in its atmosphere. The quiet comes from its enclosure, and the order from its formal, well-balanced layout. This is a place you want to spend time in, to hide away from the noisy city outside and just enjoy.

In both house and garden, the mix of old and new has been cleverly managed, neither infringing on the other, each with its own boundaries. The garden would have been completely different had it been opened up or the approach to the rear changed. The modern garden works well with the house, but the jewel of this garden is its secret, and keeping the two areas separate has maintained the sense of otherworldliness of the cloister.

ABOVE: A reflecting pool brings the water right up to the house and helps to overcome the change in levels.

OPPOSITE TOP: Though it is not old, the water cistern looks completely at home on its plinth in the centre of the parterre.

OPPOSITE BOTTOM: Looking out from the house, there is little to hint at the secret garden that lies beyond.

TOP: The transition between modern and old has a strong geometric pattern punctuated by phormiums, but softened by liriopes.

ABOVE: Lollipopped bay trees (*Laurus nobilis*) provide year-round definition.

LEFT: The soft, airy planting within the sharply definedborders of the parterre is summed up by this golden oat grass (*Stipa gigantea*).

ABOVE: Lavender along the path looks great and, with its strong scent, appeals to children.

Scented plants

Just as you might want different flowers at different times of the year, so you can plan to have different scents coming and going as well. Though sometimes you need to get very close to flowers to get the full effect of their scents, this is exactly what children do, and it is a joy for them to smell different things in the garden.

There are some plants that even our old noses can pick up, especially if they are in a semi-enclosed space. If you plant more than one of a particular type and put them somewhere you are going to get very close to – for example, by a seat or doorway – you have more chance of catching the scent.

Following is a list of plants that smell particularly good at different times of the year:

Spring
Viburnum x juddii – a deciduous shrub with highly scented white flowers.

Burkwood osmanthus (*Osmanthus* x *burkwoodii*) – a large evergreen shrub with fragrant white flowers in spring.

Armand clematis (*Clematis armandii*) – an evergreen climber with scented white spring flowers.

Summer
Butterfly bush 'Black Knight' (*Buddleia davidii* 'Black Knight') – this might be a weed, but the flowers smell of jam roly-poly and attract butterflies by the hundreds.

Lavender (*Lavandula angustifolia* 'Hidcote') – the most quintessential summer scent.

Rosa 'Madame Alfred Carrière' – for scent, climbing roses around a door or over an arch cannot be beaten. This one has creamy white flowers.

Winter
Elaeagnus x ebbingei – great for an evergreen hedge enclosing an area, this has tiny scented flowers in early winter.

Winter honeysuckle (*Lonicera* x *purpusii* 'Winter Beauty') – not a pretty shrub, but its winter flowers smell beautiful.

Sarcococca hookeriana **var. *humilis*** – this member of the box family can be used, like box, to add structure or make a hedge. It has a wonderful advantage over box in that it has incredibly strongly scented flowers in winter.

Extra Large

XL Introduction

In very large gardens, there is space to create completely different areas with completely different ambiences. Wildflower meadows, formal gardens, ponds and swimming pools are all possible. In the Drama and Hedges garden, there is even space for a green theatre, and in the Seating and Water garden there are four different types of water: a natural woodland stream, a rocky stream, a pond and a swimming pool. All of this can work in a single garden precisely because there is room to separate each of the features so that none imposes on the others.

The very large gardens featured in this section tend to be more expansive and more connected with the landscape around them. Views are often a part of the garden scene, and this informs the feel of the garden. In the Country Estate garden, the main lawn has been formed to draw the eye down the valley and to the best views. The nature of the surroundings, however, can impose restraints on what can be done within a garden. Where the Mature and Mellow garden runs out to meet the countryside, it would be inappropriate to put in man-made structures to compete with this, and instead a dome of willow integrates perfectly.

The spatial division in very large gardens can be more grand and imposing. Walkways can take on a meaning of their own: you can create an avenue of trees to guide you around the garden, and an allée of hedges, as in the Drama and Hedges garden, is an experience in itself, not just a path.

These gardens also tend to be final destinations: they are not just staging posts, they are *the* family home and garden. So many family memories are likely to be bound up in them, so many years of change and growth; gardens like these develop and mature alongside children and become almost part of the family.

And because they are usually very long-term gardens, there is time (and space) to do something really special that will outlast you and give your grandchildren pleasure: plant trees and woodlands.

Planting trees or woodland

Adding trees will give pleasure for decades, provide shade and wildlife environments, and change the entire context of the garden. Where there is room, a woodland can provide a wonderful atmospheric addition to the garden. Ten years might seem a long time to wait, but looking back it will seem like no time at all, and will give you a great sense of achievement in that you will have created a wonderful environment that will improve further with age.

If possible, use native trees – trees that are indigenous to the area will be happier in your soil, will look more natural, and will be suited to the local wildlife (for food and habitat). And a walkway through the wood is pretty essential, so it is probably a good idea to put this in at the start. Using a natural material like bark chip will make sure it does not jar with its surrounds.

Planting distances

Normally you would look at the spread of a tree after 5 or 10 years to make sure it has room to grow into its position. Native woods do not work like this; trees butt against each other or are spread out, seemingly randomly, though the purpose of

this is to use up the available light. So if you want to appreciate the individual form of your trees, a woodland is not for you, as their canopies will mesh together.

Randomness in planting is quite difficult to achieve: one way to do it might be to throw stones about and plant the trees where they fall (with a little intervention if six have fallen together).

Ground preparation

Ground preparation really pays dividends. The trees will shoot away much faster if there is no competition for water. So removing grass and perennial weeds from where you will position your trees could make the difference between waiting 10 years or as long as 15 for a good coverage.

Tree size

The smaller the tree that is planted, the better it will get established. So putting in little two-year-olds (called whips) will give stronger, taller plants in the long run. It will also save money, as these young trees are relatively cheap. And they will look more natural; nurseries tend to remove lower branches of older trees. Time can be saved by slit planting smaller trees, which means you do not need to dig a big hole. Slit planting is just putting a spade in and making a cut in the ground. Drop the plant in so that it is at the same depth as it was previously (you will be able to see where the soil was on the stem), and firm up the soil around with your boot. You do not need to be too delicate with this: leaving the soil loose creates lots of air around the roots and the plant will not do well, or may simply fall over.

Bare-root plants rather than container-grown are best at this size as they are cheaper and will establish more quickly. Bare-root trees are available during the winter when the leaves are off and the plant is pretty dormant.

Maintenance

I very rarely stake trees, whatever size they go in at, and you certainly do not need to stake smaller ones. The natural movement they make in the wind helps to strengthen their stems and build up their root systems.

If you have rabbits or deer around, a simple spiral guard will keep them off young trees.

As mentioned above, it will make a huge difference to how the trees grow if they do not have to compete for water with weeds and grass. You can get mulching mats that fit around the tree to let the water through, but which also keep down weeds. Otherwise, you can spray around the base or take off the weeds by hand.

Once the woodland starts to get established and forms a canopy, it is possible to do some underplanting with woodland plants and bulbs. A deciduous woodland is often too dark for anything much to grow underneath once the leaves have appeared, but spring bulbs can use the light before the canopy closes up. Snowdrops and winter aconites look great early in the year, followed by bluebells and wind anemones later on.

ABOVE: More space means different areas can be created, and gives more scope for exciting walkways between them.

Extra Large.01

Ecological
Owner-designed with Justin Bere
Kent, 1998–2005

I do not think I have ever seen a garden that has been thought about so carefully and detailed so well. This is a stunning garden and everywhere you look there are delightful touches. From the industrial-looking water butts to the massed planting of hostas by the pool, it has been developed with an artistic sense and an eye for detail.

The garden has emerged from a collaboration between the owners and the architect Justin Bere, of bere:architects. 'We were originally called in to look at restoring the orchard with its collapsed walls and possibly put in a swimming pool, as long as this could be achieved without wasting fossil fuel,' says the architect. This latter point was very important to the client, who wanted a carbon-neutral garden. Justin goes on: 'Gradually the plans and the work extended to creating the whole garden to a master plan worked out by the client. It was a true collaboration as we worked together to create the garden.'

Although this is a modern garden, it works so well because it yields to history and does not confront it. It is a contemporary garden that takes its inspiration from the great gardens of the past. Old ideas have been reworked to fit with modern life, but the essence comes from the traditions of English country gardens. To coin a phrase, modern gardens can be formed by evolution, and not revolution. This careful building on history has led to a garden that appears much older than it actually is, and fits with its English-countryside surroundings. This fitting in, this feeling that the garden is just right, is also enhanced by the use of local materials for much of the garden. Combined, the design and use of traditional materials has achieved, as Justin says, 'a sense of place'.

Designer's tip In a country garden like this, so strongly entwined and connected with its setting, it is worth researching local stone and crafts and discovering what the local, traditional architecture is. Using these vernacular idioms will result in a garden that connects to its surroundings.

The barn at the centre of the garden was converted in the late 1990s to create a large house that sits on top of a rise. Ideally, the owners would keep the garden as open as possible to make the most of the views from here. But, cleverly, the owners realised that this position, on a rise just inland from the sea, was prone to some windy and quite unfriendly weather. As a result, instead they have enclosed many parts of the garden and kept the views as surprises. The views are enhanced by being framed, and the garden is infinitely more exciting for having different areas and 'rooms'.

The main garden to the rear of the house is contemporary yet based on a traditional layout: a central lawn surrounded by deep flowerbeds. Topiaried yews form a central avenue leading down from the rear of the house. This sounds much grander than it is; there are only three pairs of yews and the distance they cover is not great.

Designer's tip To make the vista from the house appear longer, the yews are placed closer and closer together as they go away from the house, creating a false perspective.

The beds surrounding the lawn are filled with a mix of herbaceous planting and shrubs that come into their own in

DESIGN BRIEF
- Keep out strong coastal winds
- Mixture of modern and old
- Ecologically sustainable

FEATURES
- Vegetable garden
- Swimming pool
- Pleached avenue

June. Clematis, irises, alliums and hebes provide a colour scheme based around purples and yellows. Over to one side is an avenue bordered by lollipopped amelanchiers, which in spring give a beautiful blossom and turn gorgeous shades of red in autumn.

Beyond this main part of the garden, and separated from it by a wall, is the swimming pool and orchard area. Between these is another avenue, continuing the line of the yew pyramids with pleached hornbeams (*Carpinus betulus*) with a beautiful curved seat at the end.

The wall between the main garden and the orchard and swimming pool looks ancient, but is in fact newly built. Second-hand bricks bedded in a traditional lime mortar with gritty sharp sand give a mellow texture. The wall's design is serpentine, curving back and forth as it makes its way around the garden. Traditionally this has been called a crinkle-crankle wall, a design that dates back to the 1700s. It was originally used for growing fruit, but the curving pattern means that it is much stronger than a straight wall and can be very tall, just one brick thick with no buttresses to spoil its curving line.

This crinkle-crankle wall surrounds the swimming pool on two sides and gives a wonderful contrast to the spectacular modern pool. The flooring surrounding the pool is polished limestone, which gives a clean modern look to the design. As Justin says: 'The limestone is the modern layer on the "old" brickwork of the orchard.' This really shows how materials, rather than the underlying layout, can affect whether a design seems modern or old. If the reclaimed brick had been continued around the pool edge, it would have had a quite different feel. Lighter, smoother, sharper-edged materials laid formally immediately give a crisp, modern feel.

The pool area includes some wonderful details. The pool is sunken into the area and enclosed by walls and the pleached trees, so appears nestled into the garden rather than added on to it. The limestone steps down to the pool level are mirrored within the pool, under the water, and at the top end is a limestone 'grille' on the ground where water enters the pool. The horizontals of the grille are wide enough to walk on, so you can walk over the water. 'These are intended to bring the water on to the land. It developed from an earlier idea of a sandy beach at the edge of the pool,' says Justin.

At this end of the pool, behind the grille, is a minimalist built-in seat that provides a full stop to this side of the area. At the other end is a 'floating raft' of decking that has the very practical purpose of hiding the pool cover. A path runs down one side and the pool appears to continue under this. There is actually a divide here, and on the far side of the path is not a continuation of the swimming pool, but a fish pond.

The pool is heated with solar panels, which are also used all year round to heat domestic water, and contribute to underfloor heating in the winter. Justin explains: 'During spring, summer and autumn, the solar panels produce so much heat that this becomes the sole form of heating for the pool. By the end of May, the pool typically reaches 80°F.'

The whole is a beautiful, almost Mediterranean mix of old and new that works wonderfully well. The strong white lines of the limestone, softened with planting, give a great contrast to the rustic surrounds.

Outside the pool, on the other side of the wall, is a secret seating area. From here there are views across towards the sea and, closer to home, badgers to watch in the woods.

On the far side of the house is the vegetable area. Again, this is enclosed to give protection from the strong winds. Entering, past two pine trees, you get a real feeling of walking into a different world. This area has a very different, quiet, secluded atmosphere to it. The beds and flooring are made with materials reclaimed when the barn was converted, so the area looks like it has been here for

ever, but is in fact only a few years old. In the centre is an olive tree (*Olea europaea*), down one side a row of mulberry trees (*Morus nigra*), and down the other whitebeam (*Sorbus aria*).

Designer's tip Olive trees are fine to use in most areas of the UK. It is not cold they object to, but sitting in wet soil. If you want to use olives, before planting dig lots of gravel into the soil to help with drainage.

The raised beds are made from old timber from the barn, and on the ground old bricks have been used to create patterned paths. The bricks have been set into the ground and left unpointed so that small plants like Corsican mint (*Mentha requienii*) can colonise the gaps.

In many ways, this is a garden of quite extreme contrasts. A modern old garden — one based on history, but designed for modern living — it uses old and new materials in the same setting and is geared up for modern concerns about fossil fuels. But what is striking is its sense of rightness. Nothing has been crassly imposed on the landscape and the modern touches have been carefully balanced with the old.

OPPOSITE: A line of yews defines the walkway across the central lawn.

BELOW: The structure for the vegetable garden was formed out of materials left over from the barn conversion.

ABOVE: The terrace, looking out over the garden, is a sunny spot for sitting.

RIGHT: Around the outside of the crinkle-crankle wall, a path winds its way back up to the garden.

OPPOSITE: The outside dining area looking out over the pond.

OVERLEAF: Viewed from the main lawn, the modern lines of the swimming pool contrast with the soft planting and old walls.

ABOVE: The wide steps below the water mirror the steps above, and look wonderful as well as providing a safe entry for children.

Swimming pools

Swimming pools, once the preserve of the rich, especially those rich enough to live in a warmer country, are becoming more popular for family gardens. If they are heated, their use can be extended at both ends of the summer, and they are pretty much guaranteed to make your children very popular.

From a design point of view, the problem with swimming pools is that they are a large, flat area (of water), surrounded by another large flat area (for sitting). Getting this to fit and blend into a garden is a challenge.

Practical considerations:
- The pool should be in the sun for warmth, but maybe with some shade around it.
- Try to keep cooling winds off the surface of the pool, to help the temperature of both the water and swimmers.
- If the pool is away from the house, you may need a changing area and you will probably need somewhere to store equipment and furniture.
- There will probably need to be sitting areas around the pool.
- Heating the pool will make it more useful, and for that you will need more equipment.
- Wide steps and a very shallow shallow-end will make the pool easier and safer for younger children.
- Lighting is useful, both for safety and for night-time swimming.
- Most pools do not require planning permission, but it is best to give your local planning department a call just to check on regulations.

Design considerations:
The pool and surrounds are large, flat areas and it is best to balance this with uprights – walls, planting or a pool house will all help to balance the composition. In the garden here, the pool area is surrounded by walls and lines of trees, and its formal shape mirrors these. However, to avoid it looking too stark, the edges are softened with planting. Any uprights you put around a pool not only help with the look of the area, they also tend to give shade and shelter from the wind.

Pools do not have to be rectangles. They can be made in almost any shape and can mould themselves into a garden. One of the first things to decide is whether you want a formal pool or an organic-shaped one. Here the formal layout of the surrounding walls dictates a formal-shaped pool. A garden with less structure would fit a less formal one.

Extra Large.02

Country Estate
Robert Barker
Devon, 2000–05

This house and garden in Devon have undergone a complete transformation. The house is south-facing, and the views down the valley are wonderful. Everything in the design stems from this.

The house was rejigged and extended so that all of the private rooms are now on the south side, and a private garden has been created just outside the house to make the most of the views. Previously the driveway went straight up to the front of the house, but this was moved and now sweeps around the garden and approaches the house from the side. Robert Barker, the architect who designed the garden, changed the approach 'to provide a private space at the front of the house. It's a working estate and I wanted to create a sanctuary at the front, away from the mud of the farm.' The space this has opened up in front of the house has been formed into a modern garden, yet one that does not impinge on the rural outlook and feel of the place.

Just outside the house, the land has been raised up to form a flat lawn, level with the front door. But rather than a traditional rectangle, the lawn goes to a point and the sharp angle aims straight down the valley and draws the eye towards the best of the views.

Raising up this plateau has increased the usable space in the garden, but also created a quite a steep drop around the sides. The drop has been formed into a sloping bank, and to discourage children (and adults) from falling down it a watercourse has been put in around the perimeter of the lawn. This is a form of watery ha-ha that is a magnet for children, who splash along and wade through it, and is shallow enough to be quite safe. The water enters the rill at one end of the terrace where it falls in a sheet down the short drop. It exits at the far corner, falling in

stages through small pools. Using a rill like this is both unusual and practical; it has saved the view from railings or walls.

In an inspired idea, the rill is lit at night to give a red glow to the sharp edge of the lawn. Robert used the water to form a sharp line: 'I wanted to articulate the edge of the lawn and create an artificial night-time horizon. We looked into all sorts of technological lighting ideas and, in the end, found a rope light from the local garden centre that works perfectly and at a fraction of the cost.'

Around the sides of the plateau, concrete slabs face the slope, but do not retain the mound. The soil is held in place by geotextile plastic mesh. Though perhaps unintentional, the concrete blocks are a great climbing area for children, who zip up and down them.

The lower area around the plateau holds a wonderful 'modern' glasshouse that nestles beneath the sweep of the driveway. Though it looks contemporary, as Robert points out it is just a reworking of any glasshouse you would find in a Victorian walled garden. Sheltering against a south-facing wall, what would in the past have been formed with many pieces of small glass has now been formed with large sheets: 'I designed it so the glass sizes are the largest we could get easily; any bigger and the costs would have risen enormously.' Unusually, yellow has been used for the construction: 'It's a working farm and this shade of yellow mirrors the industrial colours of the tractors. The glasshouse is constructed with all of its working parts on show, so the colour follows through with this industrial theme.'

The glass along the front and rear of the curve forms vents that open and close automatically with temperature

---

DESIGN BRIEF
- A modern country garden
- Reconfigure the space
- Create private areas away from the farm

FEATURES
- Glasshouse
- Rill
- Folly

changes and, in winter, the interior is heated by a small water heater that feeds four large copper pipes bent around the back wall. With raised beds and an area for seating, it provides a wonderful hideaway that even in the winter is warm and dry.

The reddish render on the wall behind the glasshouse has been created by mixing local red sand into the render to give an earthy colour, creating a modern look but one that fits in with the local vernacular.

The rest of the lower walled garden is enclosed by what looks like traditional dry-stone walling, but again with a twist. The walls curve in and out of a line of trees (newly planted, though in future years they will hold their own next to the wall) in a manner reminiscent of modern Land Art. Also, and again a wonderful cost-saving idea, they are not built entirely of dry stone. They are formed with blockwork and the stone is bedded into the mortar on the surface of the walls.

Throughout the garden are a number of wonderful little touches for children to enjoy. At the top of the steps, from the lawn down to the glasshouse, are two spyholes built into the wall at child height. Further down the steps, the wall has been slit to provide a place for looking through and for playing bows and arrows. And the grass outside the glasshouse has been formed into a series of undulations for children to run over and roll down.

Around a little further, on the lower level, is a folly. It is a small building with curving steps up to a platform. To a child this could be a fort or a fairy castle, or just somewhere to sit. To the adult eye, it is a very sympathetic structure that enhances, rather than detracts from, the design.

Designer's tip Follies are one of the best examples of the joint adventure of modern family gardens. They are exciting to both adults and children, and can easily work with any design rather than fighting against it. Let your imagination wander and all sorts of structures become possible. They can also (although this goes against the pure idea of a folly) be useful. Stairs up to a platform can house storage underneath.

There are two main themes to this garden that are truly interesting. The first is the way new and old are juxtaposed and blended. The terrace and house front are incredibly traditional, and the lawn could be traditional too – except that it is not symmetrical and goes to a point, giving it a stylishly offbeat feel. The glasshouse in the walled garden could also have been very traditional, but by using larger sheets of glass and allowing the construction to show in a semi-industrial way, it has been transformed into a modern sculptural building.

The other theme is the small details that have been so carefully thought about. The spyholes and the undulations on the lawn for the children, the lighting of the rill at night, the way the glasshouse rises above the wall behind so that vents can catch the air – details like these take a good design to another level.

LEFT: Water enters the rill around the lawn from a gap in the wall around the stairs.

OPPOSITE, TOP LEFT: The wide lip means the water makes a pleasing, heavy noise as it falls into the rill.

OPPOSITE, TOP RIGHT: Inside the glasshouse, the rising curve is accommodated with shallow, wooden steps.

OPPOSITE, BOTTOM LEFT: The rill around the lawn is a magnet for children, who can paddle or use it for Pooh sticks.

OPPOSITE, BOTTOM RIGHT: The folly appeals to both adults and children.

ABOVE: Rising around and up, the glasshouse blends organic with manmade materials.

LEFT: The lighting makes the most of the long, rendered walls.

OPPOSITE: A beautiful, snaking wall runs alongside the driveway.

ABOVE: A watery ha-ha acts as a barrier at the edge of the lawn.

BELOW: The south-facing walled garden looks very modern, but is a reworking of a tested theme that appeals to both old and young.

Glasshouses

Most of us, when we think of glasshouses, think of a conservatory, which is for sitting in, or a greenhouse, which is for plants. The former is fine, but is really just a sunny room. And the latter is also fine, but is just a place to grow plants. Something somewhere in the middle, as in this garden, is much more exciting. Plants are used to create atmosphere and, even in the middle of winter, there will be greenery here as well as the scents of the flowers. But it is also a place for sitting and enjoying.

This glasshouse takes its inspiration from the orangeries of the 18th century and Victorian conservatories – places filled with plants, but designed mainly for people to enjoy.

If you are thinking about growing plants 'under glass', temperature is a major consideration. To grow really exotic plants, the temperature should be a minimum of 13°C (55°F), but in summer ventilation and shading will be required to prevent the glasshouse from becoming too hot.

In addition, glasshouse plants need constant watering during the summer, and some also require moist air conditions. This can be achieved fairly easily with an automatic watering system and a humidifier. But all of this water will mean that the floor should be washable, and you should also avoid soft furniture.

Warm glasshouse plants
- For scent: Madagascar jasmine (*Stephanotis floribunda*), jasmine (*Jasminum polyanthum*), wax flower (*Hoya carnosa*)
- For fruit: Mandarin orange (*Citrus reticulata*), lemon (*Citrus* x *meyeri* 'Meyer'), grape (*Vitis* 'New York Muscat')
- For structure: tree fern (*Dicksonia antarctica*), bamboo (*Fargesia nitida*). scarlet banana (*Musa coccinea*)
- Smaller plants: aluminium plant (*Pilea cadierei*), orange monkey flower (*Mimulus aurantiacus*), spider lily (*Tradescantia* Andersoniana Group 'Osprey')

RIGHT: The vents in the front open to allow air to circulate on hot days.

Extra Large.03

Mature and Mellow
Owner-designed
Gloucestershire, 1985–2005

This is a true family garden. It has developed over many years and has been added to again and again. The family moved here nearly 30 years ago and the garden has developed and grown as the children have moved on through childhood and adolescence. And it is an interesting example of what can be achieved if you are thinking of being in the same place for a long time. The tiny seedlings of silver birch put in 20 years ago now tower 20 metres (65 feet) in the air. Hedges are mature and the wildflower meadow well established. Tiny plants that were just dotted around have now grown and form a mass of colour and texture.

Designer's tip When planting, think about how soon you want to achieve a finished look. If you want an instant effect, position the plants closer together and overfill the borders. You will have to thin them out over the years, but at least you will not be looking at bare soil for several seasons. Alternatively, if you want a garden to mature over many years, and if cost is an issue, be careful not to overfill the beds with plants. Find out the size of the plant at maturity and leave enough space for it to grow. In practice, a middle way is usually best. Overfilling the beds slightly will give you a decent spread in a year or so, but will not be out of control in five to seven years' time.

There are two ways to get a really good garden, one that works for you and that you enjoy. The first is to have it designed to your specification, and this way is ideal for an instant effect and a garden where everything works immediately. The other way is to mould the space over time, adding to it and developing it as your needs change. The latter is what we have here. It is a garden that has been used and loved over many years, and so has the ambience of 'enjoy me', not 'look at me'.

When the family moved in, there was no garden to speak of and the house was a wreck. As the house took shape, the spoil from the building work had to be deposited around the garden, which created interesting mounds and slopes. Over the years, different areas have come and gone. One from the 1970s remains: a sunken seating area with shiny, dark-red engineering bricks that must have been the height of fashion, but this now sits slightly forlornly as a relic of garden history.

However, this development, over time, also shows how old and new can fit together. The large herbaceous borders are unremittingly traditional, but offset by shiny metal sculpture and entirely modern sitting areas.

Because it has been changed and adapted as the years have gone by, there is now a layering of features and details in this garden that you would not find in something more recent. It holds the history of the family.

There is a garden room bordered by hedges with a wooden central stage surrounded by planting. This used to be for the children: the two girls acted out their plays in this miniature theatre. The elements are still here, but now it is a meditation area with a Buddha in the planting. The high hedges provide an enclosed area that is quiet and restful, and perfect for its new purpose.

Another feature that previously would have been for play is now also for adult contemplation. The willow dome at the far end of the garden is perfect for sitting and looking over the wildflower meadow. And in the circular nature of

DESIGN BRIEF
• Quiet sitting areas for meditation
• Designs that tell stories
• Wildflower and wildlife areas

FEATURES
• Willow structure
• Deep herbaceous borders
• Modern sculpture
• Wildflower meadow

things, the children, who are now grown up, have laid claims to it as a place to get married.

As the family's needs have changed, space has been created for very modern touches. At the entrance to the house, the owners commissioned a piece of sculpture from garden designer Paul Cooper, which is based on Ingres's *La Source*. Water, representing life, winds across a slate path and falls into a still pool. Above the pool are two carefully balanced stones – Yin and Yang – which, when touched by nature (a bird landing on the structure or just a breeze) tap the still water and create ripples.

This idea of storytelling through gardens is not new – allegorical gardens are an established feature of garden history, and this can add a different dimension to garden design. It moves beyond meeting people's needs and creating a pleasant space, to become art.

This garden is not about plants or prettiness, although the plants are beautiful and the garden magnificent. It works on a deeper level and shows that gardens are intertwined with people and families and their stories. Memories are created in gardens and stories are told through them. And because of this history, the garden itself takes on a meaningfulness that helps us to appreciate the passing of time and the nature of the world.

OPPOSITE, TOP LEFT: Slates laid on their edges make a textured path for water to flow along.

OPPOSITE, TOP RIGHT: A lovely detail of three stones carefully placed on top of each other.

OPPOSITE, BOTTOM LEFT: Sculpture pieces like this one are positioned throughout the garden.

OPPOSITE, BOTTOM RIGHT: The garden sculpture based on Ingres's *La Source*. Water flows from the slate channel into the pond, and the stones, when touched, gently tap the water, causing ripples.

OVERLEAF: The wildflower meadow with the willow dome at the rear.

ABOVE: In the most traditional part of the garden, deep herbaceous beds flank a stone path.

ABOVE: A modern sitting area designed by Julie Toll.

RIGHT: In what could have been a neglected ditch, the owners have created a hidden walkway surrounded by shade- and damp-loving plants.

BELOW: Traditional herbaceous beds full of irises and foxgloves give a country-cottage feel.

LEFT TO RIGHT: The huge willow dome, designed and built by Ewen McEwen; Looking up inside the dome the willow reaches towards the sky; Windows have been created to look out over the wildflower meadow.

Making willow structures

The willow structure in this garden was designed and built by Ewen McEwen. It is a very large structure which, for the time being, requires a metal frame to keep it in place. Smaller willow structures are surprisingly easy to make and provide a natural play area or sitting area for the garden. It is a great way to get children involved in the garden: not only can they design their own feature, they can also help to make it. Carole Hockey from Wildworks, which designs willow structures and supplies willow rods, points out that they are 'also good for wildlife, supporting insects and animals'. Carole finds that 'everyone likes this fresh green space that's enclosed by willow; it feels lovely to be sitting amongst the trees'.

Willow structures are made using willow branches (called willow rods), and you will also need a tool to make planting holes for the rods – a crowbar or strong metal stake – and ties to hold together the weave. The rods are supplied during the winter, and this is the best time to build the structure.

Willow is amazingly versatile and will grow in pretty much any ground. It will do best, however, in full sun and reasonably good soil.

It is possible to make interlocking tunnels, windows, doorways, niches and domes – all using the basic construction method outlined below. A tepee for little children is a great way to get started.

Willow rods
Generally, the Internet is the best source for rods. And the best willow is *Salix viminalis*, as its branches are straight and pliable. For most structures you will need one-year-old rods. If you are creating larger structures, use two- or three-year-old rods for the uprights and year-old ones for the weave. Once you have got one structure, the cuttings from that can supply you with additional rods for extensions.

How to create a basic tunnel
- Plant uprights every 10 to 40 centimetres (4 to 16 inches) along the sides, using the metal stake to make the holes, which need to be about 30 centimetres (12 inches) deep.
- Between each upright, plant two diagonal rods so that they cross as near to the ground as possible and will cross others further up the structure.
- To create the tunnel, tie together the uprights to form a series of archways.
- For additional strength, weave in

one-year-old rods along the sides and tie them in where necessary. These rods will eventually die, but by that time the new willow growth will have taken over their role.

Carole Hockey suggests that preparing the ground – clearing the weeds – will give the willow the best start: 'Membrane does the trick, but doesn't look very good – it's better to just weed around the base for the first year. After that they will be able to cope on their own.'

Maintenance
If it is dry in the first summer, water occasionally. And each winter, tie in shoots that can add to the structure and cut off any unwanted shoots.

Extra Large.04

Drama and Hedges
George Carter
Norfolk, 1993–2005

You might look at this garden and like it, but assume you do not have the space to create something similar or, indeed, 50 years to let the hedges grow. However, though the garden here is quite large, it is not as big as it might seem. It is almost a hectare (2 acres), but the land surrounds the house so the available space on each side is limited. What is more, the ideas used in it can be transferred to almost any size garden.

George Carter, the designer and owner of this garden, moved in 12 years ago. The oldest, tallest hedges date back to this time, but the planting has continued over the years, and some of the hedges are just five years old or less. So it just takes a little patience.

The garden is almost completely green and the hedges form a strong architectural structure. They are used, as George says, for 'spatial organisation'. This is a distinct approach; George sees garden design as about the architecture of space and the spaces here, enclosed by green hedges, make up this garden, each leading on to the next and connected by allées and walkways.

There are very practical reasons why this design works here. As is typical of Norfolk, the land is flat, and the rooms give interest and a vertical dimension to the garden. They also shield the house and the garden from the prevailing winds. The enclosing hedges hark back to a long tradition in garden design where the garden is seen as a haven away from a dangerous world. In this enclosed garden, nature is tamed, safe and tranquil. The feeling of tranquillity is enhanced by the symmetry of each room and the way the gardens and vistas align and work together to form a continuous narrative around the garden.

And, of course, all of this was carefully planned. It is imperative to have a solid plan to get these walkways, openings, hedges and avenues to come together. Like any wall, a hedge is not easy to move, so you need to be sure when you have got your plan that you are going to stick with it. The layout here began with the viewpoints from the house, and the design makes the most of any length in the garden to create wonderful vistas. As you move around the garden, you are led from one focal point to the next, and everything integrates beautifully. But overall the plan is quite simple. George has divided up the gardens into rooms, very much like the ground plan of a house, each with its own feel and purpose.

Designer's tip Hornbeam (*Carpinus betulus*) has proved particularly successful in this garden and the most tolerant of the extremes of weather here. George put in small plants, but more closely spaced than is usually the case. Planted very close together, 'they grow up, rather than out, and a hedge of 3 metres (10 feet) high is not difficult to achieve'.

My favourite room is the theatre. Based on an Italian design, two rows of hedges form a semicircle around this area. The inner hedge has niches cut out of it, which means children can run in and out, between the hedges, and there is a ready-made stage for them to perform on. Box balls (*Buxus sempervirens*) in a line represent the lights along the front of the stage.

Moving away from this open space you come to a long, thin walkway running alongside it, with an urn at the end. The contrast in feeling here is enormous as you walk

DESIGN BRIEFS
- Formality
- Enclosure
- Architecture

FEATURES
- Hedges
- Ornaments
- Green theatre

out of the sun and into the shade, away from openness to a feeling of being enshrouded in green.

Beyond the walkway is an orchard that has been given a sense of order by planting a semicircular hedge around it and a smooth grass walkway through the centre. Looking back from here, the entrances are lined up perfectly with the urn in the central niche of the theatre.

Through another entrance, the garden opens up once again in the form of a large lawn, the focal point of which, lined up with the house, is a 3.5-metre-tall (11.5-foot-tall) flint obelisk. This is the central feature of the rear garden, and the final crown in the view out from the house. Closer to the house is a parterre with santolina drifts enclosed in box hedges. The eye is drawn to the more distant obelisk by side flats of hedges and trelliswork.

Designer's tip While the hedges are growing, a temporary trellis framework around them will give immediate geometry until the plants are mature.

At either side of the lawn are trellis pavilions that provide seating and reinforce the symmetry. The pavilions were made quite easily from timber and trellis and have a very stately appearance.

The buildings and ornament in the garden are mischievous and fun, positioned, decorated and painted similar to a stage set. Each object is carefully sited to be discovered or to mark a view. Many of the pieces were designed by George, and are not always what they seem. On closer inspection, the urn, set on a plinth, is a plywood cut-out, and a golden orb on top of a lead water feature is a spray-painted ballcock.

Designer's tip There are more than 50 objects in this garden and so much ornament can work because they are not seen together. George screens them from each other by placing them in niches or framing them with planting so they do not overwhelm the garden.

The water feature sits centrally at the front of the house. The plan here, though still regular, is quite different. The floor material changes from grass to gravel, giving a much harder, less cushioned feel to the area. The gravel has been used to create beds enclosed by fencing, but is less formal than elsewhere, with rosemary and lavender spilling over the sides. In the garden, the main planting palette is, as you might imagine, limited, with just yew (*Taxus baccata*), box, hornbeam (*Carpinus betula*) and lime trees. One surprise is *Phillyrea latifolia*, an olive-like Mediterranean evergreen that does actually thrive in this cold Norfolk garden, its smooth, dense, dark-green texture responding well to shaping.

This is a modern garden, but one that takes its inspiration from the formal gardens of the 17th and 18th centuries, with references to the classical. According to George: 'The simplicity and geometric planting of the past goes well with modern tastes for the minimal and the architectural.' And on top of this formality is a layer of whimsical ornament that prevents it from becoming sombre. This is a garden to be enjoyed, to have fun with and in. Walking around it, the sense of discovery is delightful, the hidden corners and adventures into the unknown a joy for both adults and children.

ABOVE: Next to the house, drifts of santolina are enclosed within low box hedges (*Buxus sempervirens*), while at the rear a tall flint obelisk catches the eye.

OPPOSITE: At the front of the house the floor surface is gravel, which gives this area of the garden a different feel.

ABOVE: Ornament, much of it the work of George Carter, abounds in this garden, but with each piece separated from the next they do not complete with one another.

LEFT: This parterre, at the front, is held in with low fences rather than hedges.

OPPOSITE: Follies and ornaments adorn the garden and add a sense of theatre.

ABOVE: A water feature made mainly of lead is topped off with a gold-painted ballcock.

LEFT: An Italianate urn, sitting in a niche, is finished off with a gilded lead star.

BELOW: One of a pair of trellis timber pavilions flanking the main lawn.

ABOVE: A hornbeam (*Carpinus betulus*) hedge with cut-out niches forms a green theatre, with box balls (*Buxus sempervirens*) to the front representing stage lights.

Hedges

Hedges do not have to take for ever to grow. So if you know you are going to be in the same property for at least five years, it is worth thinking about using hedges to divide up the garden and create interest.

You do not have to stick to using hedges around the edges: curves and swirls, circles and squares are more fun. And you can create little rooms, one of the best examples of which is the quiet room at Anglesey Abbey, a National Trust garden near Cambridge. It is formed from silver berry (*Elaeagnus* x *ebbingei*), an evergreen that has the most wonderfully scented flowers in winter, which reached above head height only four years after planting.

Richard Todd, head gardener at Anglesey Abbey, offers the following tips on planting hedges.

- The best time to plant hedges is in autumn and winter. Decide where you want them to go and use spray paint or a sand line on the ground to get a good curve or straight line.

- Choose the plant to suit the job. If you want screening, an evergreen hedge might be best, something like yew, elaeagnus, laurel or a small-leaved privet like delavay (*Ligustrum delavayanum*). If you want changes through the year and perhaps more light let in during winter, deciduous plants like beech or hornbeam are a good choice. Hawthorn will give an informal look or, alternatively, a small-leaved evergreen like yew gives a very good, formal, straight line.
- Choose the plant to suit the ground. If your soil is very wet, avoid yew; laurel would be a better choice. If heavy, avoid beech; hornbeam will do better in these sorts of conditions. Box and yew both do well in shady areas.
- Very fast-growing plants will need trimming up to three times a year. To keep down the maintenance work, use plants that do not romp away: yew, box and holly will only need cutting once a year. Most hedges, cut after the second week of August, will have no extra regrowth that year.
- Preparing the ground needs to be done only once: do it right and you

will be rewarded with a strong, fast-growing, healthy hedge. Remove weeds and dig up the earth to loosen the soil, not just where the new plant will go but also where its roots will explore. Dig in lots of well-rotted compost.
- Buy larger plants if you want a more instant effect. It is usually best to buy small so that they establish well, but larger plants may be necessary if time is short.
- If you do not have time to keep weeding around the hedge, lay a semipermeable membrane around the base of the plants, or a good layer of mulch to keep the weeds away.
- Any plant in its first year in the ground will need help with water in drier weather, and hedges are no different.
- Feed your hedge once a year in the spring. Pelleted chicken manure is a good organic feed.
- If you want a dead-straight top edge to your hedge, put up string along where you want to cut and use this as a guide. Tie in supporting upright poles at 4-metre (13-foot) intervals to get the string really taut.

Extra Large.05

Seating and Water
Cheryl Cummings
Herefordshire, 2004

This is a country garden with a good supply of large trees, so even though it is only a couple of years old it has the height and maturity of a more established garden. The site also has a natural stream running alongside it, which the owners wanted to be able to sit next to.

There is a lot of water in this garden: two ponds, the natural stream and a swimming pool. But, because it has been elegantly designed, by Cheryl Cummings, the different types of water fit seamlessly together and what has been created is a garden with several areas of very different character that together form a coherent picture.

The garden has a natural flow to it as it arcs around the house, with curving paths and sweeping lawns interspersed with planting. The water helps to hold the design together, rather than being an add-on. 'The client's main requirement was to link the garden together as a whole – to make it cohesive and interesting,' says Cheryl. Key to achieving this are the bold lines of the lawns, paths and the abundant planting.

At the side of the house is a terrace with a pond right next to it. The water has been taken right up to the terrace so that the slabs slightly overhang the pond. Cheryl says: 'The idea is that when you look at the pond it has the illusion of going right under the terrace.' Rocks and pebbles have been put under the stone of the terrace to make the transition from hard standing to water, and for the very practical purpose of hiding the pond liner.

On the other side of the pond, the grass stretches right to the edge of the water. This is a great way to create a curving edge to a pond – a line that is strong, but natural. The pond liner is tucked under the grass, which is something I had always imagined would be bad for the grass as it would not be able to form good roots and would go yellow in summer. However, the opposite is the case: the grass forms a wick effect and takes water from the pond. The slight downside to this is that the grass right next to the pond is slightly mushy, but this does not affect how it looks or grows, and the effect of grass next to the water is very attractive.

Designer's tip Rocks, both large and small, are a great friend in the garden. Around ponds they can hide pool liners, mark edges and create 'beaches'. Large stones can be used as seats or play areas and, set into the ground, whether amongst trees or in the lawn, can be good enough to pass as garden sculpture. Cheryl is very keen on using rocks and stones in the gardens she designs: 'They're great for disguise, low maintenance and really good for wildlife. And because large rocks and stones are robust, they're great for family gardens. They are also relatively inexpensive, look natural and will age beautifully.'

This pond is fed by a rocky stream from a slightly higher pond. Different sizes of rocks and pebbles have been used to create a natural-looking stream flowing around the lawn. And across this lawn is the swimming-pool area. It has been sectioned off with deep-planted beds, and the wide entrance is defined by planters. The planting around here is very important, as it helps to bed the pool area into the garden so that it does not look like it has just been plonked there. Planting is always a great way of both defining and blending different areas. If you have a patio, a summerhouse or a climing frame that you want to

DESIGN BRIEF
- Different areas that flow together
- Wildlife
- Water
- Sitting areas

FEATURES
- Swimming pool
- Pond
- Natural stream
- Vegetable area

look like part of your garden – plant around it. Immediately it will seem integrated.

Along one side of the garden is a steep-sided stream. The brief here was to be able to walk and sit alongside it. Cheryl's solution is ingenious and beautiful. A staggered wooden boardwalk steps up and down and corners in and out alongside the water, creating a stunning effect. This demonstrates how decking can best be used. It has provided flat, usable areas where the ground is uneven and falls away sharply leaving no room to sit or walk, and gives a strong line without grating against its natural surroundings.

Designer's tip The wood here is not decking wood, but treated timber planks. These give a much more natural, slightly uneven and more worn appearance. If you are using decking, it is worth considering treated timber planks if you want a more 'lived in' look.

Cheryl also wanted to increase the noise from the water so she put more stones (stones again) and pebbles into it to enhance the babbling-brook effect. She has also supplemented the planting in an unusual way. Hostas, candelabra primulas and woodland shrubs would usually be planted alongside natural streams. But here Cheryl has also put in some large architectural plants, such as phormiums and grasses, that work very well and stop the planting looking too bitty. This is a great example of creating a truly separate, special area of a garden. What was an overgrown stream has been transformed, and is separated from the rest of the garden by thick planting. Together, the

overhanging trees, water and boardwalk create an atmosphere of quiet tranquillity.

The proportions of this area are different to the rest of the garden – it is almost a tunnel, and the light, filtering through the trees, immediately lets you know that you have entered another world. Here, you could be deep in the countryside.

Around to the other side of the house is a lovely vegetable area. It is simple in layout and construction, but, once again, it is the details that make it work so well. There are four large, raised rectangular beds around a smaller, central, square bed, and their proportions and the paths between them are just right. If the walkways were too small, the area would looked cramped; too large, and it would look empty. The beds are formed from dark railway sleepers. On the ground is a light-coloured gravel that contrasts well with the sleepers and gives a clean, modern look to the area. Along the front of the raised beds are different varieties of thyme that provide year-round greenery and soften the lines of the sleepers. A tree in the central bed gives height to an area that might otherwise be quite flat.

Water is the major theme of this garden, and where there is water there are areas to sit. Integrating water and seating is often a difficult design task, but here has been carried out skilfully. The trick is to suit the seating area to the feel of the water and to think about how the flat surfaces in the seating area and the water will interact. On the terrace, a natural boundary that is not too contrived has been achieved by allowing the flags to overhang and making the transition with stones, avoiding a hard line that would look too manufactured. By the swimming pool, the seating area is enclosed with wood and has decking on the ground. These clean, straight lines and the modern feel fit perfectly with the straight lines of the pool. And by the stream, the effect is that of a wild garden, with the sitting area and walkway completely in harmony with the loose planting and woodland-walk feel of the area.

The design was also about making the most of what was there naturally. The stream has been enhanced in subtle ways with planting and extra stones. The huge trees have been incorporated into the design. And the garden flows with separate, yet integrated, areas that are joined together with paths and planting.

LEFT: A perfect use of decking, above water and surrounded by plants.
The decking provides a usable walkway where the land is too steep for a path.

ABOVE: A stone seating area appears to jut out over the water.

LEFT: Across the lawn, the swimming pool is hidden behind planting so does not compete visually with the natural-looking pond.

BELOW: Stones and rocks help to ease the transition from patio to water, and hide the lining of the pool.

ABOVE: The swimming pool and pool house sit within deep-planted beds that help to provide shelter and soften the large area of stone.

RIGHT: A dry-stream bed provides a visual link between two areas of water.

BELOW: In the vegetable garden sleepers are used to form raised beds.

ABOVE: Chives provide seasonal colour along the front of the beds, while different types of thyme provide year-round greenery.

Edibles

Food from the garden is a wonderful thing – it is healthy, educational and it tastes better. But if you are busy, and if your garden is small, it is probably way down on your list of priorities. I used to have an allotment and a greenhouse; now I have a family.

However, I do still have three strawberry plants, half a dozen lettuces and a courgette. Where before I grew many things from seeds, I bought these from the local garden centre as young plants. But it is better than nothing, and my children can watch and wait for the strawberries to ripen, or pick the courgettes and then eat them for tea.

Unless you are going for self-sufficiency, it is not quantity that is important. So start small. If the plants do not die and you do enjoy the produce, next year do a little more. If you're not a keen gardener, the worst thing you can do is to make a huge patch that you feel you have to fill – this will just be a chore rather than a pleasure.

Tips for starting out
- Unless you really want to spend time on gardening, do not create a large vegetable and fruit area. A hole in the planting or a container will do; treat them as you would annual bedding.
- At first, buy small plants rather than grow things from seed. This is not the most economic route, but it is less work and more likely to succeed.
- Put the plants somewhere that gets some sun, is near the house (so you do not forget about them completely), and somewhere that can be watered easily.
- Strawberries are my number-one plant for non-gardeners. They do not need work, the flowers are pretty and the produce is very popular. I like to grow my own lettuces, too, as you can be sure they have not been sprayed or treated. You can also buy different colours of lettuces that look quite pretty together. Sweetcorn is great to watch, as it grows so high, although whether it produces anything or not is dependent on the summer weather.

And if you decide to do edibles in earnest:
- A separate area means you can keep an eye on everything at once, and specially created beds will help to organise it. But it can be pretty. A potager can have seats, fountains and ornamental plants, like box or thyme, around the edges that keep it looking good all year round.
- Creating raised beds means you can monitor the quality of the soil that goes into them and make sure it does not have too many weeds in it.
- Paths should be just over a metre (3.2 feet) wide if you want to get a wheelbarrow down them. A good size for beds is just over a metre (3.2 feet) square, so you can reach in without standing on them.
- Traditionally, plants have been put in dead-straight rows so you know exactly where your vegetables are and can weed between them more easily.
- It is good to give children an area of the vegetable patch where they can grow their own plants. At first, expect to do most of the work yourself, but it will still be their carrots that they eat for tea and their pumpkins they make into lanterns at Halloween.

PS

Public Spaces

PS Introduction

Any space can provide inspiration for gardens, whether it is a mossy glade in a wood, a shaft of light coming through stained glass in a church, or a city-centre square. If you watch and listen carefully you can absorb what makes the place special and re-create it in your own garden. Often places like these are too large and too grand to reconstruct wholesale, and you have to think beyond the scale and identify the individual elements that can then be transferred to your garden.

Inspiration like this, which is intended to give character to a space, transports gardens to another dimension – they stop being an arrangement of hard and soft landscaping and begin to take on 'a sense of place'. This is a phrase much used by garden designers, but its meaning is difficult to pin down. One way to explain it is when everything in the garden is pulling in the same direction to form a whole and unique entity with a distinct soul.

The natural world can impinge on our well-being and affect us in ways that the built environment just cannot. Somewhere, deep down, everyone has the ability to be transported and soothed by nature. And this is an effect that can be re-created in gardens because every element can be manipulated to touch all of our senses. Light and shadow, colours and textures, the scents of the garden, the feel of the ground beneath your feet – a complete experience of the garden can be created to influence and inspire. When gardens do this, they have their own essence, their own sense of place.

Because all the elements of a garden have to work together, this identity cannot be entirely imposed on a space – it has to arise from what is naturally there. If imposed, it becomes a pastiche that our finely tuned senses can spot as fake. Clues to a garden's identity come from the planting and the land around it, the nature of the soil and the topography of the ground.

The public spaces in this chapter offer inspiration that goes beyond the mundane arts of gardening and garden design. Pensthorpe, the Cass Sculpture Foundation and the Gardens of the Imagination all take their surroundings – the natural environment – and build on them to create a sense of place. The landscape, whether deep woodland, a steep hillside or open fen, is used to inform the gardens and their overall narrative.

ABOVE: At the Gardens of the Imagination, water jets, designed for elegance and allegory, are wonderfully appealing to children.

ABOVE RIGHT: This planting at Pensthorpe provides a magical, multicoloured environment for little ones.

The three gardens mentioned above also have something else in common; none is in any way designed for children. But, because they are exciting and offer many different experiences, they appeal to children as well as adults. This is what this book is all about. Children do not have to have special, fenced-off areas that may be unappealing to adults. If you create a wonderful experience, if you use your garden to its full capacity and tackle the design with excitement, the result is a garden that appeals to all ages.

Designer's tip If you take children out, whether to the woods or to a sculpture park, watch what they enjoy and how they interact with the environment. Every child is different, but you can identify whether your child likes dens and enclosed spaces, likes jumping off things or likes exploring and discovering – all of which can be incorporated into a garden.

The exception to this in this section is the Sensory Garden in County Durham, which is specifically designed for youngsters with autistic spectrum disorder (ASD), who need to be given strong clues as to what to do and how to play. But even here the joy of the garden is one that can be appreciated by all the family and that works as a garden as well a therapy area.

Public Spaces.01

Gardens of the Imagination
Dordogne, France

The Gardens of the Imagination (Jardins de l'Imaginaire) was conceived by the American landscape designer Kathryn Gustafson as a narrative tale, a journey through space and time telling the history of mankind through the history of gardens. Each element has meaning and resonance. Water is used as the symbol of life, and box bushes (*Buxus sempervirens*) for their healing, protective properties. But beyond, or should I say riding above, this depth of symbolism are some great ideas for gardens.

The garden is on a steep slope overlooking the ancient town of Terrasson and, while few of us have such a good view from our own gardens, the way the gradient is used to its full extent is instructive. Water continually falls down it in different ways; sometimes in a lazy channel, sometimes over steep steps, effervescing and dancing into life and sound. Elsewhere, still, the gullies are narrowed deliberately to force the water to speed up and bubble over the edges of its channel. And, towards the top of the slope, a stately canal runs regimentally across the hillside, emphasising the curves of the land with its bold line.

If you have a slope to your garden, you can use water in any of the ways described above: water can drop, rush, drizzle, meander or make a ceremonial descent. However, you will need a large sump for the water at the bottom and, depending on how high the slope is, the pump may have to be very powerful.

Water is also used in the main trump of this garden, this time in spouting jets – a great idea, especially for children, and so simple. A flat courtyard area is covered with water jets that emerge from the ground and rise to different heights. You may only have space for one or two, but on a grand scale like this the effect is a dashing, dancing world of water. This water feature is not just something to be admired, but also to walk amongst and interact with. The area is large enough to have a pathway running through its centre, and it is a wonderful feeling to be part of the show. Standing in the centre of the jets, everywhere you look water is caught in the sun, and in every direction there is movement and sound.

Designer's tip If you have small children, make the jets variable. The ones in this garden were a little too large and daunting for mine, and they preferred the puddles on the ground. A jet 90 centimetres to 1.2 metres (3 to 4 feet high) would have suited them better.

Cobbles on the ground allow the water to drain into central gullies. Where the path goes over these, the flow of water separates into a dozen channels, divided by stone, so you can walk over it and the little ones can quite safely race sticks down the narrow channels.

There is another wonderful idea up here, which, when I first saw it, I was not impressed by at all. But closer up, all becomes clear. It is a shallow pool with very fine sprays of water squirting in all directions. Though it does not look much from a distance, as you walk past colours appear in the mists – they are rainbow-catchers.

Down the slope, you walk alongside the ubiquitous water, through enclosed allées and covered pergolas down to the wood and to one of the most beautiful pieces of modern sculpture. The golden metal thread that winds its way through the trees is inspired. (Inspired, in fact, by Ariadne in the labyrinth.) Shafts of sunlight reflect off it to light up the dark of the woods. It is wide enough to catch the shadows of the leaves as they flit about above, and its movement, through the trees, is elegant and peaceful.

The path forges a direct line through the wood. If a tree is in the way, it comes straight up through the path. The contrast of the straight line and the natural, haphazard world around it is quite startling, bringing each feature into focus and emphasising the qualities of both.

Designer's tip The paths are of crushed limestone, the sort of thing you get in French *boules* parks. It is a self-binding gravel with a lot of fine material in it that helps to compact it in place. This is useful if you do not want gravel thrown about, and beautiful for its light-reflecting qualities. Breedon's golden amber gravel is one of the best known.

Finally, the amphitheatre, set into a dip in the hillside, is a work of art. The seats are curved in organic patterns reinforcing the stepped lines of the grassy bowl. If your children are at all dramatically inclined, something like this could be a wonderful stage on which to put on plays and act out their fantasies.

LEFT: Water rushes over steps and across a path, the channels of which are perfect for children to mess about in.

BELOW: A canal slowly drops across the land, making a bold statement.

OPPOSITE: Gold thread loops its way through trees – a beautiful piece of art.

ABOVE: It is not just the big show of water that appeals; tiny trickles that catch in rock pools, though more subtle, are just as interesting.

LEFT: A steep flight of steps allows the water to fall and gurgle, creating mesmerising sights and sounds.

BELOW: At the bottom of the slope, water is finally channelled into gutters to be recycled.

ABOVE: Fast-moving water with obstacles in its path will create the most vigorous sights and sounds.

Water features

Water adds another dimension to any garden. When it is still, it has calming, reflective qualities; when it moves it creates life, light and sound.

There are two types of water feature – the ones you can buy 'off the shelf' and those that are made for your garden. The former are usually cheaper than the latter.

The most successful water features are those that work with the garden as part of the overall design and are not just plonked on top as an afterthought.

Think about what you would like from the water, and why you want to have it at all. Perhaps it is for the sound (do you want a calm gurgle or a rushing cascade?), for reflections, for water plants, or for wildlife.

Another way to narrow down your choice is to ask whether you want a formal or informal feature.

This will often be dictated by your ideas for the rest of the garden.

Lighting the water feature can give a lot of added pleasure, especially if it is near the house. Lighting from under the water is much better than spotting a beam across its surface, which will just highlight any rubbish on the top.

If you have a large expanse of water, think about using stepping stones or a bridge to cross it.

Also consider where the water will be viewed from and what it will be seen against.

If you want moving water, you will need a power source. But if it is a closed system, and most are, you only need to top it up occasionally.

Any depth of water can be dangerous for small children. One solution is to put a grille just under the surface of water; this can be cut specifically to fit your pond. But there is still some risk, and it might be

better to stick to a feature without standing water if there are very small children about.

Finally, it is worth planning for the future. If you want your garden to remain suitable for the family's changing needs over the years, think about where teenagers and old folk – you – might want to sit and while away an afternoon by a pond.

Public Spaces.02

The Cass Sculpture Foundation
West Sussex

Sculpture is one of those areas where the needs of children and adults can merge together beautifully. Adults can bring the unexpected, art and fun into their gardens, and children can have the most wonderful, stimulating environment.

At the Cass Sculpture Foundation the works have been commissioned specifically for their setting: 10.5 hectares (26 acres) of ancient woodland and glades. Wilfred Cass, who established the exhibition space in 1994, has made it his mission to gather together pieces from 21st-century British artists on a single site. Gathered together in this one place are works by artists such as Sir Anthony Caro, Tony Cragg and Antony Gormley. As somewhere to bring children, it is not an obvious choice, but they love the sculptures here – they come with no preconceptions about art and their reactions are immediate and wondrous.

And there is much here to take away as inspiration for your own garden. The siting of the sculpture is incredibly important. Julia Fogg, the garden designer who worked with the team that developed the landscaping, says: 'In essence we've created rooms for the sculpture by clearing trees, but we've been careful to leave the character of the woodland untouched.' Placing the modern sculpture against a natural setting immediately brings in contrasts, concealment and a scale not found in indoor environments. Nature has been used to highlight the pieces, where carefully created shafts of light have been allowed through the canopy. The overall layout, too, has been designed to allow glimpses of what is to follow, acting, as Julia Fogg says, 'as an invitation to proceed'.

Putting so many different works in one place has created its own challenges, ones that would be unlikely to affect the layout of a domestic garden. But what can be learnt from this arrangement is that the whole landscape has been rejigged to accommodate the sculpture. Sculpture or ornament needs to be seen as part of the overall design of a garden, and not something added on top, as an afterthought.

Positioning sculpture within the setting is itself an art. I asked Kate Simms, the commissioning director at the foundation, what the rules were, to which she replied: 'There are no rules. One piece we repositioned seven times before it felt right.'

There may not have been any rules, but there were some guidelines. In many ways placing sculpture in domestic settings is easier than in an outside gallery. Within a garden, the piece can have a purpose – to draw the eye, to form a full stop, to define a space. And once it has a purpose it becomes more than decoration and is more likely to work with its surroundings and not against them.

You may know, for example, what effect you want from your sculpture, and you may know how big or even what colour it should be – all of these will guide what piece you choose and where you site it. The sculpture can be made or bought for its setting, or the setting can be moulded around the sculpture. Either way, they need to work together.

So sculpture should never be an afterthought, and it can be the inspiration for a whole garden. Sir Roy Strong, in his book *Ornament In the Small Garden*, states that: 'The first principle of ornament is that it should bestow a style and identity on a garden.' Whether this is formal, modern, humorous, challenging or whatever, the key is that the sculpture fits not only with the proportions of the site, but also with its character.

Designer's tip A piece can convey different styles, depending on how it is placed. Sir Roy Strong points out that: 'A pair of clean-cut classical urns flanking an entrance will reveal a taste for tradition, but also suggest symmetry and order. The same urns, covered in lichen and moss … arranged asymmetrically in a tangled glade will call to mind very different thoughts, ones of mystery and melancholy.'

ABOVE: The Thomas Heatherwick
Pavilion.

OPPOSITE: William Furlong,
Walls of Sound.

ABOVE: William Pye,
Scylla II.

RIGHT: Paul Neagu,
Eschaton.

ABOVE: Gavin Turk,
The Golden Thread.

LEFT: Wendy Ramshaw,
Gate.

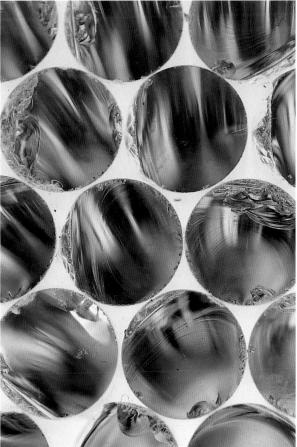

ABOVE: David Worthington,
Yo Reina.

LEFT AND OPPOSITE: Tim Morgan,
Cypher.

OVERLEAF: Sophie Smallhorn,
No 43.

ABOVE: Sophie Smallhorn, *No 43*.

Inspirations

Gardens can be beautiful and functional, yet still leave you cold. Beyond prettiness and functionality it is possible, in a garden, to create a complete ambience with its own reverberations of meaning, its own soul and character. You might believe this sort of thing is nonsense, but think of an environment that has touched you – a cathedral, a forest or a great garden. And think about the specifics of the place that inspired you, which can be re-created in your garden.

The inspirations below will not help with the layout or overall design of the garden, but are worth considering if you want to take your garden to a different level, beyond the mundane.

Contrasts
In the woodland at the Cass Sculpture Foundation, the sculptures form a contrast between their created forms and the natural surrounds. Part of their appeal is that they are unexpected, but do not look out of place. Contrasts can also be brought into a garden by using traditional with modern or bright colours in a dark place. Or the contrast can be formed by differing sizes and scales.

Scale
Many of the sculptures here are impressive partly because they are huge, and it is possible to use this unexpected scale in any domestic garden.

Light and shadows
Many of the pieces also use natural light. Glass and mirrors capture and reflect light, and sculptures with deliberate gaps or strong forms cast shadows on the ground. They form a constant upon which to mark the changing light and changing seasons.

Tunnels and narrow walkways.
Walking through narrow gaps and down corridors can make us uneasy, but focuses the eye upwards to the sky, which is framed by its surroundings.. Attention is drawn to this beautiful, ever-changing picture, which, though there all the time, may be missed precisely because it is so ubiquitous.

Labyrinths
Set paths that we walk along, without taking any decisions about which way to go, have been used for centuries as a meditative tool. In gardens, walking the same path in the same way through the seasons can bring a feeling of quiet meditation.

Large and standing stones
Large stones give an immediate impact to a garden and are tough enough to act as climbing frames for youngsters. I always find that standing stones, which you can walk between, give an eerie feeling. Stones bigger than you can make you feel very vulnerable as you pick your way between them.

Sound
If you have ever sat behind a sand dune at the beach, you will know how completely earth can deaden sound. Earth mounds and dips can create still, hushed corners.

Earth sculptures
Taking this idea one step further, it is possible to create grass-covered earth mounds and raised curves in a garden that can be turned into seating areas or dragons for children, or left as a pure clean line.

Designer's tip As long as there is access to the garden for a digger, earth sculpting is a relatively easy way to transform a garden. And if you are digging a pond or foundations, it is a money-saving way to use up the excavated soil.

Public Spaces.03

Pensthorpe
Norfolk

This garden, at Pensthorpe wetland nature reserve, is spectacular. The planting, by Piet Oudolf, falls in huge drifts that meander down to a lake in a dreamy haze of colour. It is a wonderful example of a type of planting that is becoming increasingly popular. Using mainly perennials and grasses to give hazy, shimmering movement, it includes very few shrubs. The planting patterns reflect those found in nature, where plants colonise an area, tumble over each other and blend together.

So how can what is here be used as inspiration for a family garden? Imagine you are a child and this is your garden, with bees and butterflies, places to hide, as well as the wonderful plants. If you are only 60 centimetres (2 feet) tall, you will feel like you are in the Land of Oz. For adults, there is, of course, the beauty. But these plants are also designed to be low maintenance. Chosen to fit with the environment, they need little intervention with staking, watering, feeding or pesticides. If the plant is suited to its conditions, you are working with nature and not against it, which saves a lot of labour. Piet Oudolf has selected plants that will thrive happily, work together and maintain a stable environment here. This stability also helps with weeding. Where plants are filling all the spaces for most of the year, there is little room for the unwanted to get a foothold. And this is another key idea. The plants are not cut down in autumn, as traditional perennials would be; they are left standing through the winter. Piet Oudolf chooses ones that die well, so the spectacle continues into winter with seed heads and sculptural forms. These plants can then all be cut down in one hit early in the year before they spring up again and start their display.

Leaving plants over winter also benefits wildlife, providing both food and habitats for animals, birds and insects. And this is yet another advantage of using this type of planting in a family garden: you can create your own nature reserve. Using no, or very few, pesticides and choosing plants that work with nature helps the environment. Butterflies and insects will be attracted to the masses of flowers and, once you have these, you start a food chain as birds and mammals are attracted to the insects.

Choosing plants that work with the conditions in your garden seems like an obvious idea, but it is surprisingly novel in gardening. In her garden books, Beth Chatto is the greatest exponent of this theory. Work with nature and you save yourself a lot of work and intervention that is costly both to you and the environment. Acid-loving plants will never be truly happy in chalky areas; moisture-loving plants are best kept to areas with lots of water.

Though the planting here will also work in a more modest-sized family garden, the key is to make the beds as big as possible. Rather than sticking to the traditional metre-wide (3.2-foot-wide) bed around an expanse of lawn, the beds can be the main feature of the garden. Grass paths running through them could open up into secret sitting areas hidden amongst the planting. This is natural, easy and romantic planting that Noël Kingsbury, who has written many books on planting style, calls 'enchanted nature'.

If the whole look is too romantic and unstructured for you, it can be combined, as Piet Oudolf has done in his own garden, with precisely cut hedges. These provide a backdrop for the vibrant colours, creating a wonderful contrast between the hazy planting and the bold blocks of green hedges.

FEATURE PLANTS AT PENSTHORPE
- Feather reed grass (*Calamagrostis* x *acutiflora* 'Karl Foerster')
- Coneflower (*Echinacea purpurea* 'Rubinstern')
- Coneflower (*Echinacea purpurea* 'Green Edge')
- Globe thistle (*Echinops ritro* 'Veitch's Blue')
- Joe-Pye weed (*Eupatorium purpureum* subsp. *maculatum* 'Atropurpureum')
- *Gaura lindheimeri* 'Whirling Butterflies'
- *Persicaria amplexicaulis* 'Rosea'
- *Phlomis tuberosa* 'Amazone'
- *Salvia* x *sylvestris* 'Mainacht'
- *Sanguisorba* 'Tanna'

OPPOSITE: *Sanguisorba* 'Tanna'.

ABOVE: Arranged in huge drifts, the plants create a dream-like carpet of colour.

RIGHT: *Phlomis tuberosa* 'Amazone'.

BELOW: Butterflies flutter and bees swarm around the flowers.

LEFT: Water, as well as flowers, is used to attract wildlife into the garden.

BELOW: Coneflower (*Echinacea purpurea* 'Green Edge').

BELOW BOTTOM: Grasses are used for breathing space amongst all the colour and to create a gauzy, billowing background.

ABOVE: A meadow-brown butterfly lands on a scabious flower.

Creating a wildlife garden

Messy areas, uncut lawns, fallen trees, fallen leaves and nettles are all great habitats and food sources for wildlife so, if you like to keep yours tidy, this type of garden may not be for you. The neater your garden, the less likely it is to attract wildlife. Though the mess could be restricted to the far end of the garden, even this might be too much if the far end is not actually that far away. However, there are two things (at least) that you might be able to incorporate: a pond or a wildflower meadow.

Ponds
Ponds of all shapes and sizes will attract wildlife, even in the centre of a city. And ponds do not have to be traditional either; some of the gardens in this book have very contemporary ponds – for example, rills, placed beneath walkways or cut squarely into raised beds – that are just as attractive to wildlife. If you are thinking of putting in a pond, it is important to keep down the amount of algae in the water and encourage the creatures in.

Keeping down algae
Algae are encouraged by sunlight so it is tempting to site the pond in the shade of trees – but their leaves will put lots of organic matter in the water and these nutrients will also encourage algae.

The best bet is to put the pond in a sunny position, but cover at least a third of the surface with vegetation to provide shade. In a still pond, water lilies do a great job of this.

Oxygenating plants help aerate the water and keep it clear. They come in bunches and you just throw them in with a stone attached to their roots.

Encouraging wildlife
Once you have your liner in, put soil (the poorer the better, to keep down the amount of nutrients you are introducing) at the bottom to give a habitat for pond-bed dwellers.

Make sure there is an easy point of access for animals; for example, a slope or very shallow steps.

Ideally, the pond should be deep enough so that the whole thing does not freeze in winter. To be safe it needs to be about a metre (3.2 feet) deep.

If possible, put plant cover around the edges. Long grass and dense planting will provide habitats for creatures when they are out of the water.

Wildflower meadows
Wildflower meadows have so much going for them and I cannot help but prefer them to sterile swards of grass. They are also a lot easier to maintain. I cut my wildflower area once a year at the start of September. It looks brown for a while, but grass has an autumn growth spurt and, as long as you cut before that, it will green up again before winter. Traditionally, the advice is to cut at the end of July and then treat the area like lawn, but I find my way saves a lot of mowing through the summer and autumn.

Creating a wildflower area
Though there is much debate about the right way to create a wildflower area, I have found that what works best, if you are starting from an area of ordinary lawn, is to leave it to grow and see what happens. Importantly, though, you need to have low fertility in your soil, or the thuggish weeds will flourish and the dainty weeds that you want will be crowded out.

The first year you will get lots of different types of grass with their lovely seed heads. When you cut these down, remove all the cuttings, taking away the nutrients. Continue to do this each year so that, as the soil gets poorer and poorer, you will get something different each time. Seeds that have been dormant in the soil will come through, and those from around about will come in and germinate.

This is the natural and, admittedly, slow way to go about things, but the excitement comes in the small findings. For a more immediate result, some people remove the topsoil to reduce the nutrient level in one fell swoop, and this is a good idea if your soil is particularly rich. This is the approach garden designer Juliet Sargeant takes: 'I take off the topsoil and seed it to augment the existing seeds, but I go with what's there naturally. I think it's good to have some quite instant results for encouragement.'

Some people will seed the area after spraying off what is there, an option if your soil is already poor. (If you are introducing seeds or plants, make sure they are native to your area and like the conditions of your soil.)

However you do it, a wildflower meadow will bring rewards. Juliet Sargeant always tries to encourage families to put one in if possible: 'Waiting and watching and anticipating what will come is wonderful and it teaches children to observe. I like to put mown paths through the meadow with, perhaps, a picnic spot, so you can sit amongst the grasses and flowers.' She also points out what a dynamic environment it is, always changing and getting better and better as the years go on, which is something you just do not get from a lawn.

Public Spaces.04

Sensory Garden
County Durham

The designer of this garden, Paul Cooper, has a wonderful attitude to making gardens – he just gets in there and does it. His background as a sculptor has left him with this ability to think through to the last detail how things might work and how they might be made, and get on and make it. So he was the perfect choice to design and make this highly inventive and interactive garden.

His sculptural background has also informed his design. Sculptural figures taken from the human form are quite beautiful as individual pieces. He works with blacksmiths on the larger pieces, and does the rest himself. The result is a garden that is a work of art. But it is also a design with a very specific purpose – for people with autistic spectrum disorder (ASD). People with this disorder tend to like structure, and it is important that they know what to expect and what is expected of them in a situation. Jenny Ravenhill, principal psychologist at the National Autistic Society, emphasises that the environment 'should be structurally clear, so that if someone landed from Mars they would know what to do. Different rooms with specific, expected behaviours will lessen anxiety.'

So the garden is laid out in a square, on each side of which are four rooms, each with the same configuration, arranged around a central area. Each room has four timber frames, within which are interactive exhibits, and three sculptures mimicking the human form, each designed to actively stimulate a different sense.

In the sound gallery, Paul has used bicycle bells and hooters incorporated within the wooden panels. Metal chimes hang down from the sculptures, waiting to be struck. The touch gallery contains soft planting and materials with different textures. Screens of fencing wire in the frames give a rough texture, and the sculpted figures here are clothed in smooth galvanised metal and furry, artificial grass.

In the room that explores sight, Paul has placed mirrors on the sculptures that reflect the world at different angles and, in the frames, movable mirrors that swivel around vertical poles. In a typically inventive way, the mirrors are attached to sawn-up ladder treads and the rubber feet of the ladders have been used to hide the sharp edges.

Robust plants like honeysuckles and lavenders have been used for scent, lambs' ears and soft grasses for touch, and brightly coloured geraniums and red-hot pokers for sight.

Designer's tip Children with autism have a tendency to touch and throw and eat anything in the garden, so it is best to avoid stones and pebbles, precious plants and certainly anything poisonous.

At each corner between the galleries, timber-covered 'rooms' are designed to feel enclosed and safe, and at the centre of the space a series of frames contains acrylic sheeting covered with coloured filters that are used in theatres. Walking between these frames, the world outside changes colour and looks very different. Inside the area, there is colour everywhere, and plants move across the screens in changing patterns to cast constantly moving shadows.

Designer's tip Acrylic sheets with theatrical coloured filters stuck on them were used here, rather than coloured Perspex. Acrylic is much cheaper and the filters come in a much wider range of colours.

The colours are also easy to change. This garden can be altered and developed over time to accommodate changing needs. If something works well, it can be added to; if something does not, it can be replaced. The screens set within the wooden frames in each gallery are, as Paul points out, 'also designed to accommodate experimentation – each can be changed to allow future introductions of other sensory experiences as part of the learning process.'

In a way this is a very experimental garden and, in many ways, it has to be as it is difficult to know exactly what

will appeal to its ASD users. 'No one knows what will help each individual, but if we put a range of things out there, we might strike lucky and make a connection,' says Paul.

Gardens like this go beyond merely being pleasant and into an emerging (though by no means new) theory of environmental therapy. The natural world and outside play is increasingly being recognised as a way to help people to develop and extend their range of behaviours. In a broader sense, gardens are being used more and more to help people as they can soothe and stimulate and reconnect them with nature. Even something as simple as walking on grass, hearing the wind through the leaves or watching water move through fountains can help our well-being. However, this is not a new idea, as Sir Geoffrey Jellicoe, one of the greatest landscape architects of the 20th century, has pointed out in his Appendix to Miles Hadfield's *A*

History of British Gardening: 'The Chinese laid down that the garden must have privacy and be such that its owner could commune with nature .... Here for a short time man can escape and return to the rhythms of nature for which his perceptive faculties were originally fashioned.'

ABOVE: Touching the chimes creates wonderful sounds.

ABOVE LEFT: Acrylic sheets on screens make a colourful walkway.

OPPOSITE, TOP LEFT: Mirrors can be turned and swivelled around.

OPPOSITE, TOP RIGHT: Different-coloured jars catch the light.

OPPOSITE, BOTTOM LEFT: Wire screens provide different textures to feel.

OPPOSITE, BOTTOM RIGHT: Hooters are great fun to play with.

OVERLEAF: The mirrors, sculptures and plants make this not only a place to play, but a beautiful garden to look at.

ABOVE: The different areas of the garden are clearly demarcated and appeal to different senses.

Designing a garden for a child with ASD

Every child is different, and what will work for one will not necessarily work for another. Jenny Ravenhill says: 'It's important not to have preconceived ideas about what to do; parents will know their own child and what's going to fit with that child.' She points out that children want security and confidence, and that this comes from the familiar. 'Play that's too unstructured can be stressful; many children prefer something task orientated and find this restful.'

School playgrounds can be the most awful places for children with ASD, and they see playtime as work and time inside school as more calming. 'But having said this,' she goes on, 'encouraging a child into new experiences can open them up; left to their own devices they will shut down.'

Jenny has come up with the following list of things you might want to consider for your garden if your child has ASD:

- Dividing up the garden will give clues as to what is expected; having different areas for different types of play may help.
- Anything visual is very appealing: for example, coloured lights or even just looking at the way sunlight casts shadows or comes through the trees.
- Water is probably going to be a hit. If it can spray or move, all the better, and perhaps colour the water for a different effect.
- Dry and wet sand are good, but your child may eat it and so may have to be supervised.
- Mobiles and chimes, anything that makes a noise, may also get a response.
- Children with ASD tend to be very sensitive to scents and textures. This may be a good thing and appeal, but your child may also hate them.
- Things for solitary play, like basketball or, if your child loves to ride a bike, a bike track, might work well.

- Swings and hammocks – things that move will probably be a success.
- Providing lots of opportunities in the garden may help your child. However, everything will probably need to be robust as children may, for example, damage plants or climb on a shed.

African lily (*Agapanthus africanus*).   Black grass (*Ophiopogon planiscapus* 'Nigrescens').   Mind-your-own-business (*Soleirolia soleirolii*).

Selected Plants

The plants below have been chosen to give a good spread of interest throughout the seasons, to give colour, structure and form to the garden. All have a 'modern' feel to them, are easy to grow and are 'doers' – they get on with it without any fuss. They're drawn from many of the trends that have been highlighted in the book, from the easy-to-maintain perennial border to the minimalist selection, to block or lush, green jungly planting. If you do not want to go for a pure all-encompasing 'look', these plants can be mixed together and bring their individual talents to the party. On top of all this, they are my favourite plants.

If you want a particular plant, ask at a good nursery or garden centre and they may be able to order it for you, or at least suggest a good alternative.

Short

New Zealand burr (*Acaena saccaticupula* 'Blue Haze')
I do not know why this plant is not used more. It is beautiful, grows well and is evergreen. It shoots off well from its first year to cover the ground in wonderful steely blue leaves. In summer there are red-brown flowers that turn into dark-red burrs in autumn and, with its blue leaves, this is a wonderfully colourful plant.
Height and spread:
10 x 75 cm (4 x 30 ins)

Bugle (*Ajuga reptans* 'Multicolor')
This might be too garish for some, but it is a very useful dark, low-growing evergreen that will spread out to fill a sunny spot. It has dark-green leaves with cream-and-pink markings. Small blue spikes of flowers appear in spring.
Height and spread:
12 x 45 cm (5 x 18 ins)

Mexican fleabane (*Erigeron karvinskianus*)
A very pretty spreading perennial that flops well over steps or raised beds. It prefers sun, and in summer and autumn has daisy-like flowers in white that darken to purple over time.
Height and spread:
10 cm x indefinite
(4 ins x indefinite)

Black grass (*Ophiopogon planiscapus* 'Nigrescens')
This evergreen will grow in sun or part shade. It has small, grass-like, black leaves, and tiny pink flowers in summer, followed by black berries. It spreads slowly, so if you want a good covering quickly you will need to get in lots.
Height and spread:
23 x 30 cm (9 x 12 ins)

Mind-your-own-business (*Soleirolia soleirolii*)
This evergreen will grow in sun or shade to form a dense, low mat of tiny green leaves. Frost sometimes damages the leaves, but they will come back again in spring.
Height and spread:
5 cm x indefinite
(2 ins x indefinite)

Medium

Bears' breeches (*Acanthus spinosus*)
In sun or shade, these give a dramatic performance over the summer. Their tall flowers are white and purple with large glossy leaves below. I first saw them growing on an Italian hillside under trees and the sight of the stately plants en masse was quite something.
Height and spread:
1.2 x 0.6 m (4 x 2 ft)

African lily (*Agapanthus africanus*)
These are elegant clump-forming perennials with blue-purple flowers a little like an allium, but much glitzier. They like full sun and look particularly good in pots. Flowering in late summer, they give a good boost when other plantings are looking tired. This agapanthus is not totally hardy: if you are worried about frost try *Agapanthus praecox* subsp. *orientalis*.
Height and spread:
1 x 0.5 m (3.2 x 1.5 ft)

Globe thistle (*Echinops ritro* 'Veitch's Blue')
Balls of blue flowers shoot up above the plant to just over a metre (3.2 feet). The grey-blue of the leaves works beautifully with their silvery stems, and the jagged leaves have silvery undersides.
Height and spread:
1.2 x 0.75 m (4 x 2.5 ft)

Burnet (*Sanguisorba* 'Tanna').

Globe thistle (*Echinops ritro* 'Veitch's Blue').

Eastern redbud (*Cercis canadensis* 'Forest Pansy').

Gaura (*Gaura lindheimeri*)
In mid- to late summer, these flower with a light haze of pretty white and pink. They are good just to give softness to a border and blur its edges. They prefer full sun and reach up to 1.5 metres (5 feet) tall.
Height and spread:
1.5 x 0.9 m (5 x 3 ft)

Macedonian scabious (*Knautia macedonica*)
This is a lovely low-growing plant that pushes up buttons of intense dark-red flowers all through the summer and into the autumn. Though it prefers full sun, it will also do quite well in shade.
Height and spread:
60 x 45 cm (24 x 18 ins)

Black-eyed Susan (*Rudbeckia fulgida* var. *sullivantii* 'Goldsturm')
This is a great plant for a late-summer and autumn splash. It produces bright-yellow flowers with a black cone and, even after the flowers have gone, the cones look interesting through winter, so they can be cut down in spring.
Height and spread:
60 x 12 cm (24 x 5 ins)

Burnet (*Sanguisorba* 'Tanna')
This is a perennial with wonderful, button-like, dark-red flowers that give a hazy screen pn mid-summer. It is similar to Great burnet (*Sanguisorba officinalis*), but a good 50 centimetres (20 inches) shorter, standing about 75 centimetres (30 inches) tall. It does best in full sun. The button heads look good as seed through the winter.
Height and spread:
75 x 50 cm (30 x 20 ins)

Sweet box (*Sarcococca hookeriana* var. *humilis*)
Evergreen shrubs from the same family as box, these have the most wonderful scented flowers in winter and, like box, they will do well in sun or shade.
Height and spread:
75 x 75 cm (30 x 30 ins)

Sedum (*Sedum telephium* 'Matrona')
From its first appearance in early spring, this is a lovely plant to look at and, in the autumn, it produces pink-red flowers that fade to a red-brown autumnal tone. Some say it does not need staking, but if yours has a tendency to flop, cut it back early in the summer and the regrowth and flowers will be shorter and stronger. It can be left until spring to cut down.
Height and spread:
75 x 60 cm (30 x 24 ins)

Tall

Snowy mespilus (*Amelanchier lamarckii*)
In spring, large white blossoms cover the tree, and in autumn the leaves give a spectacular display of oranges and reds.
Height and spread:
5 x 5 m (16 x 16 ft)

Strawberry tree (*Arbutus unedo*)
This slow-growing evergreen tree or large shrub prefers full sun and has white bell-shaped flowers and strawberry-like fruits in autumn. It is good for year-round greenery in a small garden.
Height and spread:
3 x 2.5 m (10 x 8 ft)

Smoke bush (*Cotinus coggygria* 'Royal Purple')
The dark-purple colour of the leaves of this deciduous bush gives a great contrast to greys and blues. In summer, fuzzy flower heads appear like smoke. If you cut it back in winter, the leaves will be larger the following year.
Height and spread:
2 x 2 m (6.5 x 6.5 ft)

Eastern redbud (*Cercis canadensis* 'Forest Pansy')
The leaves of this deciduous spreading shrub or small tree are wonderful, heart shaped and reddish-purple. It is best placed where the sun can get behind it to light up the leaves.
Height and spread:
12 x 12 m (40 x 40 ft)

Spanish dagger (*Yucca gloriosa*).

Climbing hydrangea (*Hydrangea anomala* subsp. *petiolaris*).

Climbing wisteria (*Wisteria sinensis*).

Elaeagnus 'Quicksilver'
This beautiful deciduous plant has silver-grey leaves and scented white flowers in summer.
Height and spread:
2 x 2 m (6.5 x 6.5 ft)

Olive tree (*Olea europaea*)
This slow-growing evergreen is frost hardy, but does not like wet soil. The grey-green leaves are the main reason it is grown in the UK, but you may get some olives from it.
Height and spread:
10 x 10 m (33 x 33 ft)

Black bamboo (*Phyllostachys nigra*)
This is a great bamboo for its architectural stems, and it will grow up rather than out, so is good for small spaces. Do not worry if the stems start out green – they turn black after a year or two. It prefers sun, but will be fine in light shade.
Height and spread:
 3.5 x 1 m (11.5 x 3.2 ft)

Common elder (*Sambucus nigra* 'Black Lace')
The finely cut, almost black leaves of this deciduous shrub or small tree contrast with pink flowers in early summer. It prefers sun.
Height and spread:
4 x 4 m (13 x 13 ft)

Golden oat grass (*Stipa gigantea*)
This is an evergreen perennial grass with golden flowers held high above the plant. The flowers will stay well into winter and can be cut back in the spring.
Height and spread:
2.5 x 1 m (8 x 3.2 ft)

Spanish dagger (*Yucca gloriosa*)
This evergreen shrub has long, pointed architectural leaves. In summer and autumn it has large white flowers.
Height and spread:
1.5 x 1.5 m (5 x 5 ft)

Climbers

Armand clematis (*Clematis armandii*)
An evergreen clematis with glossy green leaves and scented white flowers in spring, this shrub is happy and will flower in shade or sun. Just take off any brown leaves to keep it looking neat. It will need wires to grow up.
Height: 6 m (20 ft)

Climbing hydrangea (*Hydrangea anomala* subsp. *petiolaris*)
This deciduous climber does not need support and is great for a shady wall. It has typical hydrangea-like flowers in white, and the seed heads that form from these look good through autumn.
Height: 20 m (65 ft)

White-flowered potato vine (*Solanum laxum* 'Album')
This is the most elegant potato vine with pretty white flowers in summer and autumn. It is quite tender, so should be planted in a sheltered sunny spot. It will need support – either wires or a trellis.
Height: 5–9m (16–30 ft)

Climbing wisteria (*Wisteria sinensis*)
Its purple hanging flowers are the obvious attraction of this wisteria, but even in winter, after the flowers and leaves have gone, its stems are beautiful as they climb around their supports.
Height: 4–10 m (13–33 ft)

Star jasmine (*Trachelospermum jasminoides*)
This is an elegant evergreen climber with small, dark-green leaves. Jasmine-scented white flowers appear in summer. Although it tolerates shade, it is not entirely hardy and will do better in a sheltered place.
Height: 5 m (16 ft)